SWIMMING WITH SWALLOWS

A Taste of My Life

by

GEORGINA MALLALIEU

authorHOUSE®

AuthorHouse™ UK Ltd.
500 Avebury Boulevard
Central Milton Keynes, MK9 2BE
www.authorhouse.co.uk
Phone: 08001974150

First published by AuthorHouse 12/21/2009

ISBN: 978-1-4490-5683-4 (sc)

This book is printed on acid-free paper.

FOR DAVID

WHO MADE IT ALL POSSIBLE

ACKNOWLEDGEMENTS

My thanks go to my many friends who made positive suggestions which improved the book enormously. Special thanks to my American friends Tom Cobb and Phyllis Grannis who put me on the right path and shared their computer skills with me; Paige Warr for his constructive suggestions; and Michelle Ruddick, another American friend, for her professional editing and proof-reading.

My love and thanks also to David, Jonathan, Julian and Hannah for their constant support.

Whilst all the characters in the book exist or existed, I have changed some names where I think it appropriate.

INTRODUCTION

One of the luxuries of getting older, and there aren't many, is having time on your hands. So when I began to research my family tree I realized how little I really knew about my past. Boxes of black and white photos showed my grandparents as slightly overweight, unfashionable, and self-conscious. But I also discovered faded photographs of them in their youth, posing in front of palm trees, on sunny Indian verandahs, lounging on beaches. It looked mysterious and glamorous but who were they really, I asked myself? Who and what had been their passions, what circumstances had forged their lives and turned them into the people I knew?

How bitterly I regret all the opportunities I missed to question them whilst they were still alive. With the ignorance of the young I'd unconsciously dismissed them as simply old people who'd never loved, suffered or lived a life of any real interest. Now it is too late.

And so I decided that I should leave to our own children and grandchildren a small memento of our past. I could at least give them of flavour of the life we led as young parents, a taste of our adventures in Africa and of our final years in France. I hope they will come to understand that their parents and grandparents, who are now nearing the end of their lives, were once young and shared the same dreams and hopes as they do now.

And that for the most part, those dreams came true.

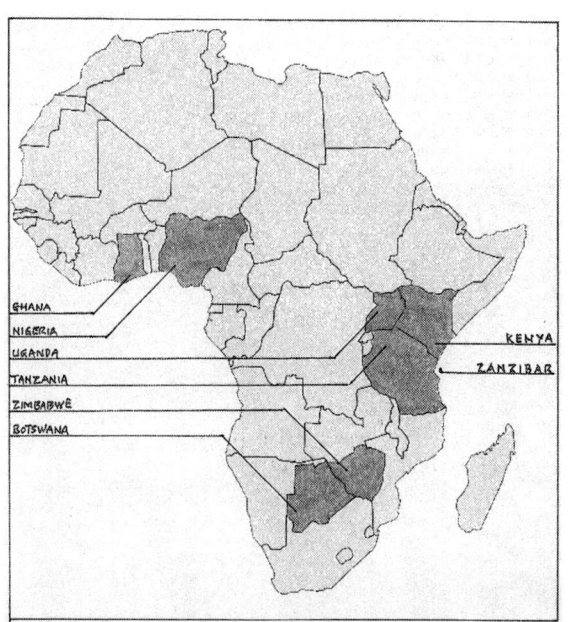

GHANA

NIGERIA

UGANDA

TANZANIA

ZIMBABWE

BOTSWANA

KENYA

ZANZIBAR

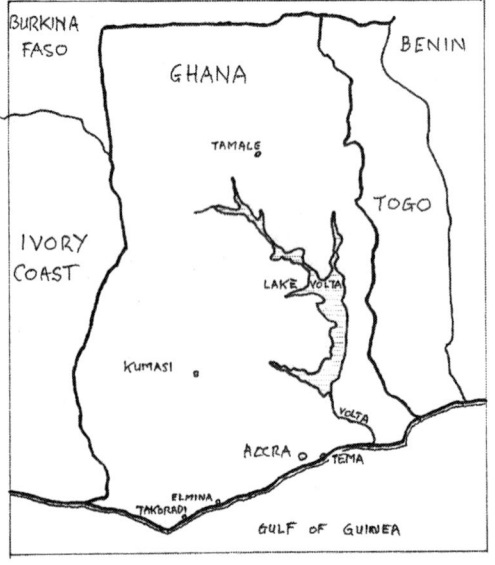

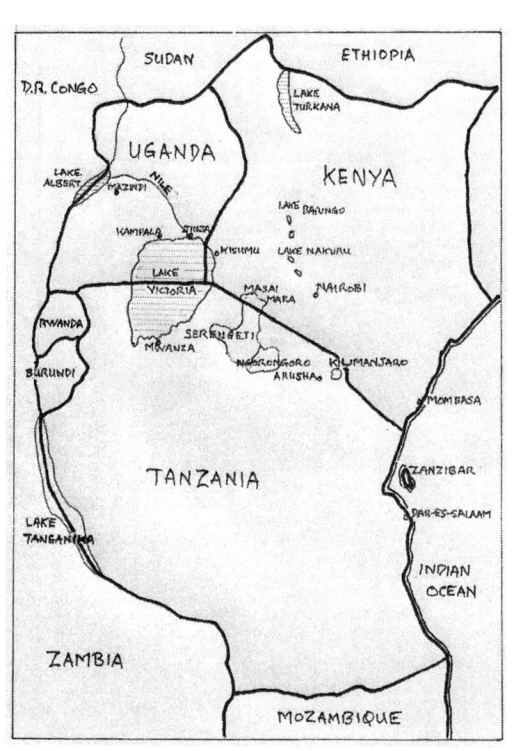

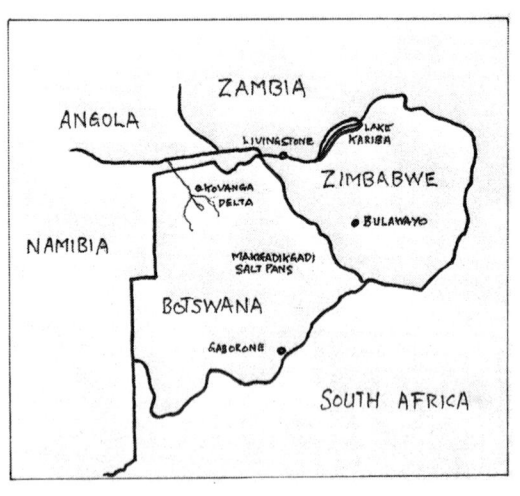

CONTENTS

1

THE GOLDEN THREAD

How strange that they too should arrive that day. As we left behind our home in England to begin a new life in the valleys of southern France, they swept in from the plains of Africa to join us for the summer months.

While we staggered into the barn to dump a lifetime's possessions, relishing the warm spring sunshine and rolling woodlands that swept down towards the river Lot, the swallows darted swiftly about our heads, swooping up into the rafters, searching for a suitable place to build their nests. I paused to watch them and at that moment envied them their freedom – not for them eighteen months of planning, packing and sorting in order to begin a new life. They simply followed their instincts, took off on their long and arduous journey and headed back to where their life began.

But hadn't we too followed our instincts? We knew it was too soon to retire, that there was no way that we could settle for the quiet round of golf , cruises and afternoon television. After a lifetime of change and challenge, of years spent living, working and travelling abroad we simply weren't ready to put up our feet. And where better to come back to than SW France, home four hundred years ago it was said, of the original Mallalieu family.

For thirty years, Africa had run like a golden thread through my life , like the swallows we had journeyed between two great continents, equally at home in both. For David it had been even longer. At the age of twenty he found himself in Ghana and then Nigeria and for the next forty years breathed, talked and lived Africa. I met him ten years after his first posting and five years later we went as a family with three small children to live in Nigeria – to the part that had been Biafra - just after the end of its bloody civil war. It was a fascinating and dangerous place – but despite all the hardships, that is where my love affair with the Dark Continent began.

For many years I'd travelled with him whenever he visited distant outposts. I saw villages and wildernesses that few European holiday- makers would ever see, experienced the best and worst of Africa – and the worst can be truly dreadful – but my passion never faltered. I kept detailed journals of each trip to read on cold dark days in England and now I smile at how often I wrote the words 'This will be my last trip to Africa'.

But the urge to travel, to explore, to rise to new challenges becomes an addiction. And that is why one foggy, frosty February morning we gazed down our Lakeland Valley and said 'Perhaps it's time to move to France.'

* * *

Over the years we had spent many holidays in France but it was only in the last five years that we had come to know the Valley of the Lot. And on that cold and dreary February day we had seen on the television the European Prime Ministers' meeting in Cahors, a town we knew and loved. As we watched them stroll through the sunny market place with its magnificent cathedral as their backdrop, we looked at one another and suddenly knew that this was where we were heading. We found pen and paper and made the first of many lists. Suddenly the adrenalin flew and the retirement that had spread depressingly before us now became a wonderful and exciting challenge.

Our daughter Hannah, who had tired of the constant commute into the City, decided that she would come with us, rent out her house, and try to make a new life for herself. So when our house search began we needed to find one with separate accommodation for her and one which would also provide holiday accommodation for our sons, their families, and also for friends. That way we could enjoy them all without losing our own independence.

And so the search began. Needless to say we saw some horrors, drove miles into the wilderness to find ruined chateaux which, had we been a great deal younger and a great deal richer, would have been an exciting challenge. We were shown derelict but still inhabited farms – and even one where the owner said he would only sell to Ernest Hemingway. I wonder if anyone ever told him….?

But we had had enough of total renovations, having already converted a cottage in the Lake District demolishing everything but three walls and then had spent a further five years putting back together a Cumbrian farmhouse. We hadn't the heart to live in chaos anymore. We needed our new home to be immediately habitable and comfortable, although we would be happy to convert or renovate the 'maison d'amis'. But at the top of our list of must-haves was land. After years of airports, hotels and offices, David needed to be out in the open air, riding his mower, cutting down dead trees and planting new ones.

We knew within five minutes of stepping into the old Quercy farmhouse, set among forty-two acres of woodlands, meadows and a small lake, that this was the house of our dreams. The main house was delightful and spacious although the 1970's renovations would have to be dismantled and a new kitchen built. The stables had been partly converted for use as a summer kitchen, where madame made all her jams, and where her husband had his workshop. The roof was new, the walls sound and the possibilities endless. There was an enormous grange where the cars, tractors, mowers were kept and whose beams were decorated with old swallows' nests. And its position in the small hilltop hamlet was magical.

During the Hundred Years War the hamlet had been in the hands of the English soldiers. The mediaeval castle and walls had been dismantled over the years by the locals in order to build their houses. But there still remained the 'porte d'anglais' – an archway precariously propping up two tumbling ruins. Later we were to discover in neighbours' homes, slits for arrows, niches for religious icons, and magnificent internal arches.

There was utter tranquility as we gazed down the oak-lined avenue which divided the two large meadows, once vineyards. Yet we were only a ten minute drive to the nearest market town with bakers, butchers, greengrocers and five hairdressers. Cahors itself lay twenty kilometers to the east with its long central boulevard, sprawling pavement cafes, mediaeval town centre, winding river and elegant shops. What more could we want? We knew there was another buyer in prospect and that he, a Belgian, was returning the following day with an architect. No doubt he saw the house and grounds as a potential holiday centre.

The owners walked us through the woods, the autumn sunlight shafting through the tall trees. The meadows fluttered with pale blue butterflies, wild flowers still dotted the landscape and across the valley the trees were tinged with autumn hues. I felt the same magic I always felt in Africa – gazing across the rolling plains to distant shimmering horizons. The sun was still warm on our faces and as I looked up, a plane, like a small silver fish, headed south towards the coast of Africa. And my heart leapt as I recalled my first visit to that addictive land, so many years ago.

2

THE DARK CONTINENT

It was in the early 1970s when our plane landed late one evening in Lagos, Nigeria. I staggered down the steps carrying Hannah and clutching the boys' hands. I couldn't believe how hot and humid it was. It was if we had suddenly walked into an enormous sauna.

"Walk quickly," I'd urged the boys, 'we'll soon get away from the heat of the engines'.

Of course it wasn't the heat of the engines at all. It was just a typical West African night. It was to take me several weeks before I could begin to adjust to the oppressive blanket of heat – although I could never come to terms with looking permanently pink and frizzy-haired.

Somewhere David was waiting to meet us, ready to take charge once again and help us prepare for the next day's journey to Eastern Nigeria. After months of planning our new life, packing up our home leaving behind only the impersonal beds, sofas and tables for our tenants, I was totally exhausted. The company were to ship out our more personal belongings such as books, pictures, and toys. We knew that there would be no schools available so I had researched home learning courses and armed myself with enough books and guides to see us through the first two years. Jonathan had already started primary school, Julian was at playschool and only Hannah was still entirely under my influence. I'd often wondered if I would make a good teacher. At the end of home schooling I awarded myself two out of ten for maths and eight out of ten for literature.

The West Coast of Africa had been known by the first explorers and entrepreneurs as 'The Graveyard of Africa.' Yellow fever, malaria and Llassa fever were only a few of the deadly diseases we might encounter. And sadly we did. We'd had countless injections, and had been armed with malaria tablets which had to be taken daily. Some years previously a colleague's baby daughter had died whilst they were posted in W Africa so we knew that we had to do everything to prevent such a tragedy happening to us. Every evening the children's bedrooms would be sprayed, their beds covered with mosquito nets which were suspended from the ceiling, and their bare skin covered with insect repellent.

I'd been alarmed by the fact the Julian had reacted badly to one injection in UK, had collapsed and had to be resuscitated and rushed off to hospital for the night. After that there could be no more injections for him so we lived with the constant anxiety of him being unprotected against many potentially life threatening diseases. But eventually I relaxed and discovered that children and old people seemed to blossom in the constant heat and humidity.

I'd learnt too that the washing must never been spread out on the ground or bushes, as the stewards like to do, as we were likely to pick up jiggers - small insects - which would worm their way into our bodies, cause a great deal of pain and discomfort and be difficult to get rid of. But trying to keep shoes on the children's feet proved to be an uphill struggle for they were happiest running around barefoot wearing only a pair of shorts. Even encounters with snakes didn't seem to bother them. In fact watching the garden boy slice off the snakes' heads was almost as entertaining to them as watching the turkeys' throats being slit for Christmas. Children are much more matter of fact about these things than we adults.

But despite all David's stories of life in Africa, the slide shows which we'd all watched eagerly, laughing at fifteen year old pictures of him as a skinny young man in shorts and long socks, I still felt unsure of what to expect. I suppose what I felt was a mixture of anxiety and excitement. When David had come home some months earlier to say that we were being transferred to Nigeria, my first feeling had been one of delight. I could never understand the look of horror on friends' faces when I told them. "How could you", they declared. "What about schools, what about doctors. Don't you think it's a little irresponsible?"

No, I didn't. Well, not at the time. Although I must admit after Julian's hospital visit and during the final frantic and lonely days of preparation, I sometimes found myself wondering what the hell I was doing. But for the most part I thought it a wonderful opportunity to see and experience a different world and culture. All my life I've jumped in at the deep end and learnt to swim. Of course I've sometimes had to be rescued, but for the most part my life has been a fantastic whirlwind of colour and excitement. I don't intend it ever to change.

After all my father and my Anglo-Indian grandmother had both been born and brought up in India. She hadn't come to England until she was in her forties. What a shock that must have been! No servants and constant cold grey weather. How homesick she must have been for the heat and the dust. She'd had to learn to shop, to write a cheque and deal with housekeeping. Apparently she had spent the first week's money on fruit and chocolates much to my grandfather's annoyance. She never learnt the art of running a home as there had always been a dozen servants to do it for her, and in her final years became known to her friends and neighbours as 'The Duchess'. At least I would be better equipped and hopefully a little more street-wise.

But what had been wonderful for us as children were the exotic tales our father told us of life in India. We were mesmerized by stories of Maharajas, gifts of rubies, tiger hunting and taking to the hills to escape the heat of the plains. Looking back I suspect these were 'stories' to amuse us, rather than fact!

Long before England became a nation of curry eaters, we children were introduced to exotic foods. On Sundays my grandmother's kitchen would be filled with the smells of simmering curries, rice and dahl. I would help make the side dishes, chopping the tomatoes and onions into tiny cubes, tears running down my face. How I had loved kneading the floury dough to make the naan and then spooning the mango and lime chutneys into small dishes before the whole family sat down to enjoy a two hour lunch. Perhaps that is where my love of cooking first began. Of course I can't remember how my grandmother cooked her curry, but tracing my family tree has put me in touch with distant cousins in Calcutta, April and Neville who inspired with me their own **Kofta recipe.***

*All recipes to be found at the end of the book

* * *

Now here I was, years later, about to set off on my own exotic adventure, to discover new foods, experience a different lifestyle and escape the humdrum routine of middle-class commuter England. I've often wondered just why I crave so much to be always moving on, seeing new places, starting from scratch. Partly I suppose it's the habit I acquired in childhood. Never staying long, constantly changing houses as my father moved with his job around the country. Becoming an observer and soaking up and storing new experiences, knowing that I would soon be moving on, became a way of life. I think I enjoy being out of my 'comfort zone' – a slight prickle of anxiety is really quite addictive. As I write I'm now in my seventeenth home. Is it the last I wonder?

* * *

As David emerged from the airport crowd to help us get through immigration and rescue our cases I burst into tears. It was a mixture of relief, anxiety and exhaustion. Getting myself and three children from our village home by train to Gatwick loaded down with pushchair and suitcases had been a nightmare.

How glad I was that David was an 'old hand' in Africa and knew the ropes. He'd already booked a room in an hotel and had installed one of the company stewards in it to 'save' it for our arrival. If the steward had not laid claim to it, our room would certainly have disappeared. Someone else would have grabbed it having bribed the receptionist. It was my first lesson in learning to be street wise in Africa.

As we drove through the dark steamy night towards the hotel I got my first glimpse of Lagos. What a strange mixture the city was. On one hand modern skyscraper office blocks had begun to dominate the skyline whilst at street level the storm drains were filled with stinking rubbish, the pavements broken and litter covered. Hundreds of makeshift stalls, lit by hurricane lamps were selling food, clothing, tools and motor car parts.

Through the open window of the car wafted the pungent smells of charcoal fires, unwashed bodies and open sewers. As we crossed the lagoon, the breeding ground for millions of mosquitoes, David told me how dead bodies could often be seen bloated and decaying, bobbing on its surface. I began to wonder if I had been crazy to bring the family out here. But maybe in the light of day, after a good night's sleep I would begin to feel more confident.

The children and I collapsed gratefully into the small bedroom we were all sharing and despite the throbbing of the ineffective air-conditioner which belched out warm air, we finally slept. At last we were all together again and our new life was about to begin.

The next morning we had to be back at the airport to catch the internal flight to Benin City, a few hundred miles to the East and from where we would be driven to our new home on the banks of the River Niger. In the morning light Lagos looked even more disturbing then the night before. The darkness had hidden much of the neglect. So many people, so many cars, so much noise. But at the same time, how colourful it was. The fabulous African prints, which David's factory was producing, would seem gaudy in any other light than this.

Here the vivid purples and yellows, reds and oranges looked magnificent against the ebony skins of the market women. Many carried their babies on their backs and at the same time balanced enamel bowls filled with their morning's shopping, proudly on their heads. It was a skill I envied.

As our small plane headed east towards Benin City I craned my neck to look out on the landscape below. What struck me most of all was the colour of the earth. It was a rust-red dusty soil which I learnt was called laterite and I was soon to discover it stained everything it touched. The children's clothes were never to look really clean but would remain permanently grimy. There were great swathes of timber rich forests whose luxuriant green foliage was mirrored in the wide meandering Benin river. Sprawling towns and villages whose corrugated metal roofs dazzled the eyes like giant flashlights in the morning sun were splattered across the baked earth.

My stomach churned with anxiety as we drew nearer to our destination. What would the house be like? What sort of environment would we be living in? Would I find any friends?

Our bags once more loaded into a car we set off for the final part of our journey along pot-holed roads, staring out at a world completely new to us. Benin City which we would explore some months later, was once the capital of the kingdom of Benin which was probably founded in the 13th century. Portuguese mariners became the first Europeans to visit this part of West Africa in 1486 and the local *Obas* (kings) established a royal monopoly over trade in ivory, pepper, cloth and slaves.

During the 16th and 17th centuries the population of Benin fell rapidly because of the slave trade and in the end the *Obas* were forced to end their export of male slaves. However they still continued to import and re-sell slaves purchased by Europeans elsewhere in Africa. In addition they also began to export palm products to Europe so increasing the country's wealth.

As a result of this new wealth the O*bas* became patrons of the arts and it was then that Benin produced some of its most famous bronze and brass castings - works of art which had their origins in the 13th century. My home now is filled with modern castings crafted in the old way – the glorious heads of the kings and Queens look surprisingly at home in the countyside of France.

However, when the British finally decided in the early nineteenth century to abolish the slave trade, the economy of Benin started to decline and the city entered a turbulent period of unrest. Surrounded by her Islamist enemies, and with her trade dwindling, the city sank to its lowest point. In a desperate measure to seek control of its inhabitants, the *Obas* indulged in a frenzy of barbaric ritual human sacrifice. From the late 1880's this horrific practice continued until the British in 1897 ransacked the city, razed it to the ground, and in so doing destroyed much of its treasures.   It is not a period either nation can be proud of.

As we neared the Niger river the children grew restless, longing to be running about after days of being cooped up in trains, planes and cars. Looking out Jonathan was amazed to discover that everyone was black. 'How long' he asked 'do we have to live here before **we** turn black?'

Finally the great iron bridge crossing the Niger loomed before us. On the other side lay the city of Onitsha, one of the last strongholds of the Biafran army. Here we were to make our home amongst the burnt out ruins, the poverty and relics of a war that had ended three years previously.

3

Big Decisions

The tiny plane had disappeared leaving a fluffy white trail across the sky, taking with it my memories of thirty years ago. Two buzzards circled lazily above the tree tops. I suddenly realized that Madame was talking to me, breaking my reverie, bringing me back to the present as we headed up the track towards the house. Would I like to go inside again and have another look? Of course I would, although I knew without doubt that this was the house we should buy. I tried to catch David's eye, and when I did nodded briefly, hoping he might read my message.

Hannah and I had already exchanged a whispered message. 'This is it!' It's difficult to define quite what instinct it is that lets you know immediately that a certain house is meant for you. But after years of buying and selling houses we knew it was important to play it calmly. But I was so in love with the house and the hamlet that I suspected that 'cool' had gone out of the window.

The limestone built farmhouse was typical of the region. Once the living quarters had been on the upper floor, reached outside by a flight of wide stone steps, whilst below were the cellars or *caves* for the animals and the wine. The whole area had earned its living from the vines until the great frosts of 1956 devastated those vineyards that had survived the phyloxera epidemic which had swept through the region at the end of the previous century.

The original inhabitants had also kept a few sheep, cows and goats and grown their own vegetables. They had been almost entirely self-sufficient. They even collected their own rain water, and when their tanks ran dry had to go down the hill to the village pump. Amazingly water was not laid on to the village until 1967.

But now the whole house had been converted into a family home. Downstairs was the large beamed sitting and dining salon, with a small room at the end, currently used as a bedroom- (I'd already decided this should be the study) - then a rather odd wasteful corridor with tiny kitchen and shower room. Upstairs was another large salon, which Monsieur and Madame called their library - which also had a large walk in fireplace - and was reached both by the oak staircase from the sitting room, and also from the stone steps and open-sided covered porch outside. A small stone room led off the porch, and this was the *souillarde*, the old kitchen which was used for plucking fowl, skinning rabbits and storing food and washing pots. It would make a great coat and boot room! There were three bedrooms and a really large bathroom.

Two of the bedrooms had false ceilings, one wallpapered in yellow and purple flowers the other in modern pine. Later we discovered beneath them both the original oak beams. All the upstairs oak floors were covered in sisal matting. It was very 1970's. But it had potential.

Although the pink vinyl flowered wallpaper and fluffy pink carpet in the bathroom would have to go at some point, at least the suite was white. It was also a large room as it had originally been a bedroom. I'd made David promise me that whatever house we bought, even if it was perfect, I could throw out any baths and washbasins which were coloured. Avocado baths were my pet-hate and I'd been forced to live with one for too many years.

I was so smitten with the whole ambiance – I think it was helped by the fact that the owners had some lovely antique pieces dotted around – that I couldn't see any major faults, except the tiny kitchen. And I was sure that could be overcome in time. Of course once we moved in I found the décor more irritating than I could have imagined. I didn't realize at our first viewing that most of the ceilings had been carpeted with moquette between the beams. Not only that but some of the walls were carpeted too. But then they say that love is blind.

We drove away saying we would think about it. A few moments later we stopped on the brow of the hill looking down onto the main village nestling on the valley floor. A small stone bridge crossed the river and the road wound around the church and village school. Here and there a chimney smoked gently in the morning sun. We could see an old man in his vegetable plot, dressed in the old men's uniform of blue dungarees and black beret. Then and only then did I dare ask David what he thought. 'Absolutely fantastic,' he said wistfully, 'just what we were looking for'.

Before setting out we had made a list of everything our dream house had to have. This house had them all except for a bakery in walking distance. We decided there and then that it didn't matter at all, and anyway it would be better for our health if we scrapped fresh croissants every morning.

I was already imagining our life in this idyllic valley. But there were two major problems. One, the Belgian was turning up the next day with his with his architect; two, we had yet to complete the deal on our English house. We'd accepted an offer from a Barrister who was desperate, he said, to move quickly and who didn't need a mortgage. This seemed to be too good to be true. And it was. He now never answered calls from the estate agent or the lawyers. When he did make contact it was to say he was too busy to sort things out. We had now reached the critical phase and he was promising to exchange within the next two weeks. But could we trust him? And if he let us down we would have to find the money for the

French house elsewhere which could make things complicated and potentially expensive.

Unlike England, the system of house buying in France is much more organized. Once you agree on a price, you pay a deposit and agree the date for completion. You can withdraw if anything untoward turns up that the seller fails to disclose. But apart from that once the deposit is paid you are committed - unless of course, you're prepared to lose your deposit.

So if we were to make any offer we would have to produce the deposit within the next ten days. Hannah and I felt that we needed to make an offer immediately and try to prevent the Belgian getting a foot in the door. We felt completely fired up. Swept along by our enthusiasm David agreed although I knew that this was a difficult decision for him as he's ruled by his head and he would much rather have had the money safely in the bank. However although I am ruled by my heart he knew that whenever I'd persuaded him that a house was the right one for us, it had always proved to be so.

But it was not the house that he'd lost his heart to, but the rolling woods, the enormous open spaces, the endless skies. I knew what delight he would take in walking through his own land. To have his own wood had been his dream for so many years. Now at last it was a possibility.

What should we offer? My feeling was that we should secure it immediately by offering the asking price. By English standards it was very good value. But David always likes a bargain and it was against his nature not to haggle a little. But I pointed out that it had a wonderful swimming pool, which had been a must for us, so we had to think of the money we wouldn't have to spend in putting one in. We finally persuaded him that ours was the route to go. Back home of course we would have organized a survey and that would mean another long delay. But the French rarely bother with them and we could see that everything was in good condition, if not always to our taste. And before the house could be sold the present owner would have had to have it certified termite and asbestos free. Monsieur C the proprietor was a retired chartered accountant and it showed in the neatness and fastidiousness of the house and the land.

So within forty minutes of seeing the house we were back in the estate agent's office ready to claim it as ours. He rang the owners, but no-one was in. My heart sank – maybe we were too late? The agent had another appointment in town and left saying that he'd be in touch tomorrow. But we stayed in his office to discuss the options with his English assistant, Liz. Ten minutes later M. Guerin returned, having bumped into M. and Mme C. He'd discussed our offer and they had agreed to sell to us! They were won over by the fact that we were planning to be permanent residents and since they were building a new house nearby they were anxious not to have a holiday centre (which the Belgian planned) on their doorstep. We learnt later that after accepting our offer, they'd had a better offer from a French couple but had decided to be honourable. Needless to say we were overjoyed.

Back at the hotel however, the adrenalin slowed and David began to feel anxious about the sale of our own house. That night neither of us slept well, because I was already busy moving in and arranging the furniture and David because he was seeing all the pitfalls. I did my best to assure him that everything would be fine and to convince him that since this was the house we'd been looking for we couldn't afford to let it slip through our fingers. I used as much logic as I could muster to win him over – I'd discovered long ago, that men don't value instinct in the same way as women. As morning finally came we both fell fitfully asleep.

Of course the first thing we did the next morning was to drive back to the hamlet to confirm that we had indeed done the right thing. Seeing it again in the warm sunshine, hearing the shriek of the green woodpecker and the distant braying of a donkey, we knew that without doubt this was the house for us. We sneaked a few photographs and then spent the rest of the morning on the telephone chasing up our English agent urging him to try to get things moving.

The next couple of weeks were somewhat stressful to put it mildly but eventually everything turned out well, as of course I knew it would. I could finally uncross my fingers. And so once again, the long journey to a new life began.

4

THE BIAFRAN WAR

It had been important for me to know something of the life
I was to lead in Eastern Nigeria and to do that I had needed
to understand a little of the history of the country. How
else could I have made sense of the poverty and destruction,
coped with the sadness and madness of the life I was to lead?
So before we left England I found out a little of the country's
history.

In 1960 Nigeria had finally gained independence from Britain.
At the time it had a population of 60 million people with 300
different ethnic and tribal groups and it was inevitable that the
transition would be stormy. In the north were to be found the
largest group, the Muslim Hausas. In the south-west were the
Yorubas, half Muslim, half Christian, whilst the south-east of
the country was dominated by the mainly Christian Ibos.

At the time of independence an alliance was made between
the leading Hausa and Ibo political parties, and they were to

rule Nigeria for the first few years. The Ibos, who were often highly educated, took most of the top jobs in the civil service and business. As a result of this East and North alliance, the Yorubas were side-lined, resulting in enormous resentment which led the Yoruba party to reform itself. Eventually they joined forces with the Hausa northerners. This new alliance was now to exclude the Ibo dominant East from power. A dangerous game of musical chairs had begun.

In 1965, this alliance of Yorubas and Hausas won a decisive victory in the elections   But following widespread claims of electoral fraud, General Johnson Aguiyi-Ironsi, the Ibo head of the Military led a successful military coup.   He appointed himself Head of State.   Like all politicians he needed to reward his supporters (at the same time protecting his back) and under his leadership the Ibos were once again in ascendance taking top roles in the army at the expense of the Yorubas and Hausas.

It came as no surprise that in 1966 there was a counter-coup led by the north and General Gowan a Yoruba, was made the new Head of State. The resulting tensions led to a wide-spread massacre by the northern Muslims of the Christian Ibos. Up to 30,000 Ibos were killed in fighting with the Hausas, and around 1 million refugees fled to their Ibo homeland in the east.

At the same time the huge oil reserves which had been discovered in the Ibo dominated south-east of the country began to generate enormous wealth. The Ibos began to fear that the revenues would go the Yorubas and Hausas leaving them neglected and impoverished.

As the Ibos saw it the only solution was to become an independent nation and in May 1967 Colonel Ojukwu, the military governor of the Ibo-dominated south-east declared that the region would now be known as The Republic of Biafra.

Civil War was declared and the Nigerian government sent in the army to recapture the region. Their use of strong-arm tactics to invade Biafra caused worldwide disapproval. But surprisingly the Nigerian army made little progress at the start of the war and soon Biafran troops led by their leader Colonel Banjo crossed the Niger river, entered the mid-Western region and launched attacks close to Lagos, the then Nigerian capital.

But a blockade of sea, land and air and a re-organization of Nigerian forces resulted in the Biafran army being pushed back into their core territories. Enugu, the capital of Biafra eventually fell to the Nigerian army. However the resolute and tough Ibos forced a period of stalemate which lasted through 1968/69. During this time the blockade turned Biafra into an humanitarian and propaganda disaster. Pictures of starving children were beamed across the world, resulting in volunteer groups organizing blockade- breaking flights into the war zone, carrying food and medicines and weapons too.

Eventually defeat could not be avoided. Colonel Ojuku fled to the Ivory Coast and the Biafran army surrendered. A million people had died in the conflict of hunger or disease. And for what? Many Biafra soldiers fled into the countryside with their weapons still willing to use them in order to find food and shelter. Bodies rotted in the long grass, homes and businesses were devastated.

Three years after the end of the war – the roadsides still littered with rusting tanks and crashed planes – we arrived to start our new life in Nigeria.

5

CROSSING THE RIVER

The journey from Benin City was fraught with tension. The children were restless, eager to see their new home. I was anxious – wondering if I'd made an enormous mistake. Looking out through the car windows I felt as if I were watching some strange exotic film unroll before me. Nothing seemed familiar. Not the landscape, the chaos, the poverty. All that was familiar was contained within the car. How was I going to adjust?

Soon the great River Niger appeared before us. Children splashed in its shallows, battered cars and lorries were being washed in its muddy waters, goats were herded down to the river's edge to drink. A huge metal bridge, partly destroyed during the war, spanned the slow-moving waters and we drove carefully across, negotiating the fragile temporary repairs.

Our house was set on a hill overlooking the Niger in the middle of what had been the Government Residential Area

(G.R.A). The old houses which had survived the war were pock marked with bullets, and bore an air of neglect. Families still huddled in the remaining corners of shelled buildings under insubstantial shelters made of plastic and sacking. The air was filled with the smell of cooking as women bent over smoking fires, roasting cobs of corn and skewers of whatever protein they could find. Rats, cats even dogs, nothing went to waste.

Our new home was a long bungalow and one of a few that had been rebuilt after the war. It was simple but at least we had water and electricity – well for much of the time anyway. Compared to what we'd just driven past it was a palace. Our compound, as the garden area was called, was fenced off from the road with two gateways which allowed cars to enter, swing around the back of the house and then leave by the second gate.

Waiting on the steps to greet us was Raphael our steward dressed in a fine uniform of white trousers and shirt. He was slender and like most Ibos, rather small. His feet were bare and his smile magnificent. He turned out to be the best steward we would ever have, although of course at the time I wasn't to know that. With him was Stan an Englishman who worked at the factory and who had lived in Nigeria for many years. With his sandy coloured hair and washed out blue eyes, Stan was the life and soul of any party. He'd supervised the rebuilding of the house which had been destroyed in the war.

It had originally been intended for him and he'd chosen the furniture and colour schemes. It wasn't my taste but it was functional and clean.

But my heart sank as I saw a huge bar, complete with pineapple ice bucket and bar stools, dominating the sitting room. It took all my charm to persuade him to take it with him to his new smaller house where it was put to great use. His marriage, I discovered later, like so many ex-patriots' in Africa had foundered – too much work, too much money, too much temptation. But all that was to change later that year when I was a witness at the strangest wedding I'd ever been to.

The large sitting-room had French windows on both sides and at one end a door led into the small kitchen where there was a fridge with small freezer compartment, a gas cooker, a water filter and a few cupboards. No foodstuffs could be left out as within minutes a trail of ants would appear from nowhere and invade the lot. I discovered to my horror that if I didn't clean down the baby high chair scrupulously after meal, it became a heaving mass of black ants within half an hour. The local flour had to be sifted carefully before use as it was full of wriggling weevils, looking for all the world like tiny poppy seeds.

We didn't have the luxury of a washing machine. Everything had to be hand-washed, if and when there was water. And when there was water it was usually a delicate shade of brown.

At the other end of the sitting-room a solid door, which had to be bolted each night for safety, led into the sleeping quarters where there were three bedrooms and a bathroom. Because they were all on the ground floor the windows were heavily barred. Seeing them brought home to me that we were indeed living in dangerous times. Stan told us he'd hired a night watchman for us who would arrive at sundown to guard the gates and the grounds, leaving at 6.00 in the morning when the curfew had been lifted.

Curfew? My heart sank even further. Yes, despite that fact the war had been over three years, the town was still under military control which meant that from 10.30 pm no-one was allowed out on the streets until the following morning. I should have felt safer but soon discovered that many of soldiers who were supposed to be guarding us, were in fact roaming the streets heavily armed and high on drink or drugs. Not only that but former Biafran soldiers who had fled armed into the countryside would occasionally make raids into town looking for food and money. You could be shot for the price of a loaf of bread. It occurred to me fleetingly, that maybe this deep-end might turn out to be a little too deep after all!

The two bed-roomed staff quarters situated just behind the house, had their own kitchen, shower and toilet. The quarters weren't particularly large but when the majority of people had no running water at all, they must have appeared luxurious. There was always a family member or two visiting, and I used to watch them pounding yams for their meals, drying their brilliant cloths on the hedges whilst bare-bottomed children chased hens around the compound.

I suppose I'd set out to Africa determined not to become a typical white *madame* employing masses of servants and idly whiling away my time. I had after all once worked for 'The Guardian'!

How different it all was in reality. People were so poor, so desperate for jobs and money that we found ourselves employing as many staff as we could afford to feed and house. In addition to Raphael who cleaned the house and helped cook, we took on Vivienne a young girl who helped with the children and Amos to sort out the garden. From time to time they would come to ask if I could find a job for their 'sister' or 'brother'. The term was loosely used – it could have meant just that, or a half- sibling, or indeed just someone from their own village. Interestingly they always wanted to work for a white family – partly because we paid better and partly because we didn't make too many demands and were generous with free time.

My first Christmas in Nigeria I'd given Raphael the day off and decided to do the cooking myself. By the time I'd finished preparing a three course meal I was totally limp and exhausted. The atmosphere was unbearable as we had no air –conditioning in the kitchen, and I had not adjusted to the heat and humidity. Raphael would have been quite happy, he told me afterwards, to have had a day off another time. And of course he would have been able to share our Christmas food with his family. For all the cooks made sure they cooked that little extra which they would be given for their own families. That was the second lesson I learnt in Africa – you had to see things through local eyes, and not assume that English 'fair play' always benefited people of another culture. Raphael and I exchanged recipes during the following year, and I hope he learnt as much from me as I from him. **Groundnut stew*** was one of our favourite dishes – easy to make and delicious to eat.

When we'd arrived the garden had been a barren waste, but the great joy of gardening in tropical Africa is that everything grows so abundantly. Within months the garden was a riot of colour – purple and orange bougainvillea hedges, pink and red hibiscus and flower beds of zinnias and canna lilies. The barren earth was planted with the coarse grass that eventually turned the dusty red soil to deep green foliage. The garden was watered from a standpipe at the back of the house and I would often see small children wandering in from the road with huge jugs on their heads to collect water from it.

When the frangipani blossomed its waxy white flowers filled the air with their heavy perfume attracting hundreds of tropical butterflies. But there were constant reminders of the war too and often Jonathan, Julian and Hannah would run in clutching live bullets which David took down and threw into the river.

The traumas of war were even more horrific at the factory which David was trying to get up and running again. The huge textile factory lay at the end of the bridge which had partly been destroyed and was now temporarily patched together. It had been the site of huge battles and the grounds and outbuildings of the factory were littered with rusty army equipment, and worse still, hundreds of skeletons. Huge skips were used to carry away the bleached bones.

Each morning the children and I set aside a few hours for study and for what I hoped was creative play. It was exhausting and frustrating for us all. As a result of my input the children developed into great readers and hopeless mathematicians! How many tears of despair I wept during those early days. I longed for some grown-up company, someone to talk to, some like-minded soul to laugh with. It was good when David was at home with us – he usually had Sunday afternoon free – but he was so busy with work, leaving home at six in the morning and getting home late in the evening. Often he was away visiting up country and became extremely thin with the work, the heat and the stress.

From time to time a couple of other European wives would arrive, spend a few weeks, sometimes a month or two and then return to UK. They were either reluctantly childless or menopausal – both depressing states of mind - and it was sometimes a struggle to find a common denominator. But as people learn to do in times of stress we were forced to bond at a certain level and found comfort in at least discussing the weather, where to buy washing powder and more excitingly, who was to be the next visitor.

There was something about ex-pat life that seemed to encourage bitterness and bitchiness. Maybe it was the loneliness, the fear of the unknown. Maybe it was because wives were so much part of their husbands' work overseas that competitiveness and status become increasingly important. Arguments would arise over the size of your air-conditioner. Had we paid for it ourselves or had the company given us a better one? Why were our wine glasses cut glass when theirs were cheap supermarket ones? Dear God, what a bore it often became.

And then of course there was the question of what to wear. Before we set out for Africa I'd asked David what sort of clothes I needed. Ridiculous question of course, he couldn't give me any idea except to say that it would be hot, so cool cotton clothes. But of course he didn't understand fashion, or style or the mores of the day. I soon discovered that we needed to change three times a day when the weather was really humid; that after six when there was any socializing the other women always changed into long dresses. I'd not taken enough clothes, that was quite clear. A hurried letter to my sister in UK who fortunately shared the same taste, resulted in a few more dresses turning up some weeks later. Then I learnt to choose some material from the market and let a local seamstress copy a favourite dress. This system worked well although the choice of material suitable for European skins was very limited. There's no doubt that having the right clothes gave me, and still does, confidence - I wish it were otherwise.

Then there was always the dilemma of visiting dignitaries. Would everyone be invited to lunch or only the selected few? Since there were only usually six ex-pats at one time it wasn't a real problem was it? But it certainly used to become one as some struggled to assert their imagined seniority.

One morning Vicky, a colleague's wife came for coffee. My age, but childless, she was a pretty woman with long straight hair, slim hips and a large bust. She had a very disconcerting habit of making no eye contact when she talked to you but gazed pointedly at your bust. At first I was would finger my shirt buttons in case I'd left them undone. Then I'd glance down fearing I'd tipped my breakfast down my front. Or was she just comparing sizes? It's a habit she never grew out of.

Having sipped her coffee she casually dropped into the conversation that someone from the High Commission was visiting next week and she'd been asked by Duncan to organize a lunch. Now Duncan was the other Englishman who shared responsibility with David for the running of the factory, together with their Chinese partners. His wife occasionally turned up in Africa, but not for long.

'Only a small lunch party' she murmured, 'inviting a few important people for him to meet.' Clearly we weren't included.

She smiled sweetly as she bit into her scone. I hoped there were a few weevils baked in it. If there's one thing guaranteed to raise my hackles it's having my husband or children, insulted or threatened.

'Really?' I smiled back. 'How nice for you.'

Not one to let sleeping dogs lie, I resolved to confront Duncan at the earliest opportunity. However we didn't meet too often and it was the day before the lunch when I bumped into him at the club bar where he was drinking with a group of out-of-work lawyers and colleagues. Whenever I saw him I always thought of the term 'lounge lizard' - perhaps unfairly. His wavy ploughed hair was always neatly cut, his large black framed spectacles dominated his small boned insincere face. I accepted a gin and tonic.

'Hear your having a lunch party tomorrow, Duncan'. I smiled innocently and was pleased to see that he looked slightly uncomfortable.

'Ah, yes, chap from the High Commission. Thought I'd take him round the factory to have a look at what we're doing.'

He turned to the others, 'Anyone ready for another one?'

I didn't let go. 'Only I was surprised that David and I didn't get an invitation.' We made eye contact and I refused to let go. He knew that I knew no invitation had been sent.

'Really, how awful, can't imagine what went wrong. Can't trust these girls in the office. Make sure you get one today. Look forward to seeing you both.'

I finished the drink and left to go home where Vivienne was supervising the children's tea. As I walked past Vicky she muttered, 'Well, you certainly know how to stir things. Buy you a wooden spoon for Christmas!'

Some weeks later I had an opportunity for revenge. Walking from the club to the house in the cooler evening air I was accosted by two young Ibos girls. 'Are you a missionary?' they enquired. I made a mental note to check my appearance when I got home. They then tried to convert me to whatever brand of Christianity they practised, offering to come to my house for Bible readings, prayers etc. I suddenly had a wonderful idea.

'That would be great. How about tomorrow, say 8.30 pm. This is my name and house address, I know my husband would be delighted to see you'. I gave them Duncan's name and drew a map of his house. We parted, each of us happy that our task was done. Unfortunately I never discovered the outcome.

In all ex-pat communities around the world you seem to find the same incestuous scandal-mongering, sexual manoeuvrings and social climbing. I've often been bemused by the enormous need to cling together, to be constantly meeting for lunch, dinner, weekends away. Is it driven by fear of loneliness, fear of being foreigners in a strange land? Or did they all live that sort of life back home?

Maybe it's just that my life has made me more independent and introspective so that now I've learnt to live with a certain amount of solitude. The truth probably is that it's me who is the odd-ball. We've met many charming and delightful people around the world but we've just learned to keep a certain distance and I know that we acquired a reputation of stand-offishness. I suppose the reality is that postings abroad are often short and that you simply can't afford to get too close to people for tomorrow you or they will have gone.

6

FRIENDS AND FOES

I t was not until I met Obi, whose father was a local Nigerian Chief and mother English, that I formed a friendship that opened up for all of us a new and fascinating insight into the local life and culture. Her husband Dada had been an officer in the Biafran army, had been shot in the legs but had survived to become a local entrepreneur. He was charming, blue-black and very handsome standing well over six feet. He was also great fun and understood the European sense of humour. Obi was also tall with that special beauty that mixed marriages so often produce. They had four small children and so at last our children found new friends too. We spent several Sundays together exploring the local countryside, picnicking in the forests, even sailing down the Niger in search of crocodiles.

One Sunday we all decided to head down the river as the children felt in need of an adventure and it would be good for us all to get away from the work environment. Although we'd heard that there were crocodiles in the Niger, we'd never seen one, so Dada arranged for us all to hitch a lift on top of a yam boat.

Yams, tubers which form part of the local staple diet, were shipped down river along with plantains – huge green bananas which have to be cooked - and various other goods for sale or barter. We loaded our cold box with **breaded chicken breasts*** (the chickens were very stringy and since they were fed on fishmeal, tasted of haddock); **home-made crisps***, as the bought ones from the supermarket were always old and soggy; fresh fruit and weevil-free homemade **fruit cake***. Fanta orange was the kids favourite drink whilst we packed plenty of beer for ourselves.

The yam boat was wooden, long and flat. It had a sturdy wooden roof which provided shade as well as covered space for the cargo. That day the roof was piled high with bunches of plantain, wicker baskets overflowing with yams and various bundles of cloth plus an old bike. Money exchanged hands and Dada loaded us all on board where we squeezed on top of the roof, tightly holding onto the children who were bursting with excitement.

We set off down river watched closely by bemused locals. I thought of how it must have been for those first explorers finding themselves in this strange new world so many years before. And despite all the hardships and the frequent solitude

I realized how incredibly lucky I was to be experiencing something so tantalizingly unknown.

After an hour the boat pulled into the bank and we clambered off, found a gentle slope to perch on and opened our lunch box whilst the owner of the boat conducted his sales. We stayed there for a time aware that we had become the centre of great interest. From behind every tree a little face would peer out bemused by three blonde children and the strange food they were devouring. An old man with a machete sat a few feet away, watching us carefully. I felt uneasy, still unable to distinguish between idle curiosity and malevolent intent. But he was perhaps more afraid of us than we of him.

But our river journey home as the sun began to sink was totally relaxing. The children had lost their boundless energy and were content to sit and watch the world drift by. Hannah lay asleep, her head in my lap, as the fishing canoes paddled their way home on the now dusky pink river. The banks of the wide slow moving Niger were fringed with palm trees, their sharply etched fronds motionless against the darkening sky.

Firelight flickered outside the village huts, and the smell of roasting meat and fish filled our nostrils. Half naked children laughed and chased one another seemingly unperturbed by the killer mosquitoes which threatened us all. Soon we would be back inside our modern house, switch on the lights, run the bath and within the space of five minutes leap forward a hundred years.

We never did see a crocodile.

*   *   *

But life was not always so peaceful. One morning, some months after our arrival I'd walked into the sitting room, leaving the children crayoning in the 'schoolroom'. To my horror I'd found a wild looking man sitting in one of the easy chairs. He was dirty and dishevelled with hair that had not been cut for a long time. I remember vividly his worn torn red shirt which looked like a huge splash of blood against the pale blue of the chair.

There was not a sound from the kitchen so I knew that Raphael must have gone to his quarters. With my heart pounding I closed the sleeping- quarters door carefully behind me, hoping that the children would stay there. The intruder stared at me through red-rimmed eyes. Smiling he said in pidgin English, 'You give me money one time'.

My heart started to pound. I knew I didn't have any on me, unless I was going shopping I didn't bother to ask David for any. But then I remembered David's words of advice 'Always smile, never get angry'.

'I'm sorry' I told him. 'I really don't have any money in the house. Can I give you some, er... clothes, some food?' I couldn't decide whether he was on drugs or drink, or whether he was mentally disturbed. Or, God forbid, all three. But either way I had to get him out of the house. I rushed into the kitchen, hoping that Raphael might be making his way back.

There was a pile of clothes by the sink ready to be washed. I grabbed a handful of t-shirts and shorts and then snatched a loaf of bread and a piece of cheese. Rushing back into the sitting room I pushed them into his hand and told him he must go. The children meanwhile were still happily playing.

Thankfully he got up and walked out of the house and made his way down the path. I locked the French window quickly and burst into tears as Raphael walked back into the kitchen. From then onwards we not only had a night-watch but a day-watch too.

But despite the fact that we had night and day watchmen there was absolutely no guarantee that they would do their jobs effectively. I'm sure they had to work both days and nights to feed themselves and their families. One night when David was away up country, I lay awake as the moonlight streamed through the barred windows. There had been a power failure and I'd been awoken by the sudden silence. Usually the groaning of the air-conditioner lulled me to sleep.

Outside I could hear the distant barking of a dog and down towards the river the faint murmuring of engines. No doubt the curfew patrol. I threw open a window hoping to catch a breath of air, pulled the mosquito netting tightly around the bed and hoped that sleep would come and with it the morning.

It had been a bad week. Just outside the town was a large hospital and on a couple of occasions we'd met some English, Canadian and German doctors who were working for a short time out in Africa. We rarely saw them but some weeks previously we'd bumped into some of them at the film night at the social club. Ancient films were projected onto the club wall and we sat on metal chairs on the badminton court. Often the reels were in the wrong order, and small lizards ran across the heroine's face while we were bitten by furious mosquitoes.

We'd exchanged a few remarks with the doctors and then settled down for 'Lord Jim'. I'd found it totally incomprehensible but then realized that it was being shown back to front and that reel four was inter-changed with reel two. At the end of the film we all had a drink together and then shaking hands went our separate ways.

A few days later I discovered that one of the young married German doctors had become ill with Llassa fever. This was very worrying. Lassa fever is specifically found in West Africa, especially in rural areas and is contracted from the excreta of infected rodents. It is also passed on by bodily fluids, and hospital workers are especially vulnerable working with infected patients in poor hospitals.

Karl, who was in his twenties and newly married, had needed a tracheotomy as his throat closed up with the facial swelling. His colleague Dietrich had performed one, but sadly it was too late and Karl died. Then Dietrich himself became infected and there was a huge operation to airlift him out to Germany with everyone cocooned in protective clothing. Some years later I heard that Dietrich had married Karl's widow back in Germany.

For a week we'd had all been obsessed with sore throats and any sign of fever. I lay in bed that night wondering if we'd been reckless to expose our children to such dangers. But then I suppose you could stay at home and be killed by a falling ceiling. A much greater threat was being robbed by drink or drug crazed locals.

I got out of bed and peering through the windows wondered where the night watch was. I unbolted the door into the sitting room and wandered silently from window to window in the dark, peering out into the garden lit white by a pale moon. I could see no-one. Finally I opened the French window and walked around the compound, clutching my dressing gown placing my feet carefully on the laterite paths hoping the snakes were fast asleep.

It did occur to me that the night-watch might think I was an intruder and machete me. Now that would be ironic. However the chances of him being awake were slight. I guessed he was in the staff sleeping quarters, flat out. I was right.

I think my yells woke the neighbourhood up, but I was mad. I've no doubt that the next night he did the same thing. But it was impossible to be angry for long – their lives were so different from ours, we had so much and who was I to impose my standards on someone whose life I could not even begin to imagine? The truth was that I liked the Ibos more than I liked most of the ex-pats I'd met.

There was only one other incident when I'd been really afraid. And that was one night when we were driving home, an hour before curfew fell. We'd been out to dinner, leaving the children with Vivienne. Suddenly a jeep full of Yoruba soldiers pulled up in front of us, causing us to stop. I wound down the window and a large rifle was pushed through the gap, its gleaming metal stopping an inch from my temple.

'Why you no home?' the soldier demanded angrily. 'Why you break curfew?' I was just about to retort angrily when David took over. 'Officer, we're so sorry we didn't realize it was so late' he smiled 'thank you for reminding us. Won't happen again'.

The gun was withdrawn and we'd hurried home arriving half an hour before the curfew began

* * *

Despite the fact that both David and Dada had heavy work commitments we tried to get together again for further family outings. We explored caves, chased butterflies for my collection (yes, I know it's now politically incorrect) and

Dada and David even managed to sink a native dug-out they borrowed.

As we watched them paddle out into a lake one leisurely Sunday, the canoe slowly disappeared under their combined weight and they were forced to wade back dragging the boat behind them. The children thought it absolutely wonderful. I'm not sure their fathers shared their delight.

Later that same day we'd come across some caves – dark damp and horrid. But the men thought they might try to explore them despite our pleas to not do anything so stupid. Our protests were brushed aside with the usual male arrogance. However after a couple of minutes trying to squeeze themselves down a narrow tunnel even they thought better of it and we all retreated outside in search of our picnic and fresh air.

Looking back I realize how simple our picnic meals were. Lack of ingredients and electrical gadgets meant that we relied on simple fresh food, simply cooked. Our lives and experiences were far less sophisticated than they are today. As I browse through my old Africa recipe book filled with snippets from favourite recipes, I think perhaps I should return to them more often. Sometimes today's complicated 'cheffy' recipes with masses of ingredients and complicated sauces are too much. Or perhaps it's just my age.

How grateful I am for those wonderful memories and how important I realize it is to throw yourself completely into the life of the country in which you find yourself. It's all too easy for ex-pats to cling together for support in face of the unknown, to hang onto old habits, seek out the sliced bread and dry-cured bacon. But what joy and what freedom it is to let it all go and to make new friends and immerse yourself in a new language, a new culture, another life.

7

ONE WEDDING
AND A FUNERAL

And so began our new life in Nigeria. Our past lives and routines had suddenly become irrelevant and now we had to start again to try to establish some pattern which would give us a sense of identity once again.

Each morning we woke to blazing skies and oppressive heat. It was only when the Harmattan trade wind blew south from the Sahara once a year that we felt a sense of relief, as the temperature dropped to the 70's and the humidity lessened. The sun would be hidden and the air filled with fine desert sand that looked exactly like autumn mist.

How the locals hated it! Raphael would come in each morning mumbling about the dust everywhere and walking around huddled in a baggy sweater. Amos insisted on working all day in his woolly hat. I tried to explain what real English cold was by showing Raphael pictures of snow and persuading him to put his hand in the freezer for a moment – he couldn't believe that anywhere could be that cold. But then he was both surprised and disappointed to learn that I didn't have tea on a regular basis with the Queen.

After breakfast the boys and I would go into the third bedroom which was now the schoolroom, and try to work our way through the books I'd brought over. Occasionally we were joined by Lee a young boy whose Chinese father was M.D. of the factory and whose Japanese mother we met occasionally for a formal dinner. It proved impossible to form a close personal friendship with either of them. Many years later I heard that Lee had gone to the States and was then an Assistant District Attorney in Seattle. Afraid I can't claim any credit for his success.

Raphael's two year old son Simon would appear in the staff quarters a couple of times a year. The rest of the time he lived up country with the extended family. As he was the same age as Hannah I suggested that he might like to come and play with her. I think Raphael felt a little uncomfortable of the crossing of barriers but he did agree that we might try. However Simon was very timid – I don't suppose he saw white faces very often. I did persuade him to come into the house once and got out the toys and crayons. But he burst into tears and ran back to his quarters. On one occasion I tried to encourage him to play in a warm bath with plenty of bubbles and toys. But he screamed so much that I never tried again. I used to watch his young cousin pour bowls of cold water over him and soap him down in the yard. He was happy then.

But as much as I loved my children I often found being alone with them twenty-four hours a day quite depressing. I was used to living in a village where when we went walking we'd often bump into someone, be invited in for a cup of coffee to discuss the local gossip. How I missed those encounters, however brief. Going for a walk in Onitsha was difficult because of the heat. Once in the first week I foolishly decided to take the children for a walk, heading towards the small social club where there was a pool. They say only mad dogs and Englishmen go out in the mid-day sun. This time it was a barmy English woman, three children and a pushchair. By the time we walked back I was so hot I stood completely dressed under a cold shower while Vivienne tipped the three of them into a cold bath. After that we only walked down in the late afternoons, suitably dressed in sun-hats and with an umbrella.

But within months I was to take part in two very memorable events.

*   *   *

Stan, who worked at the factory as head of design had become a firm favourite of the boys. I suppose that was because in many ways he was a big kid himself. He'd tell them corny jokes and play with them in the pool whenever he had time He even persuaded Jonathan to dive in the deep end by bribing him with a bottle of beer.

When we arrived Stan was living alone, having been divorced for some years. It was only many months later that I discovered from someone else, . the tragic story behind his bubbly character.

Arriving in West Africa he and his first wife, Shirley, had been swept up in the social whirl of drinking and partying. His work was demanding and exhausting but even so at the end of each day he'd find his way to the local club where, being the gregarious soul he was, he'd pass the hours laughing and drinking with his friends. But for his wife, as for so many childless wives who are far from home, it was an aimless and unsatisfactory life. That is until she met Colin a lonely Englishman living with the agony of losing his only child and first wife.

I only had the story secondhand but I believe that somewhere in West Africa some years earlier,   Colin, who had been left in charge of his two year old daughter, had fallen asleep and woken to find her body floating in their swimming pool. Who can imagine the horror, the guilt, the despair? The incident ripped the family apart and within a year his wife was dead, dying they said of a broken heart.

So when Shirley and Colin met it was hardly surprising that they   found in each other, someone who could understand their loneliness. Within a short space of time, Shirley left Stan in Nigeria and returned to England with Colin. They eventually married, and I wish I could say they lived happily ever after. But life is cruel and within months of their marriage Colin developed cancer and died shortly afterwards. Then, Shirley finding that she couldn't live without him, committed suicide.

I never heard Stan mention his wife or his past. When we met he had a busy social life, and knew all the local township bars and clubs. One evening we were introduced to a slender beautiful Ibo girl who appeared to be his latest girlfriend. She was very fashionable with her ornately plaited hair, but she was very quiet, hardly opening her mouth all evening. She fell asleep at the dinner table. Since Stan talked non-stop I suppose it was a good arrangement.

Some months later Stan announced that he and Esther were to marry and asked if I would be a witness at their civil wedding? Afterwards there was to be a celebration and traditional native marriage in her father's village, where he was the local chieftain.

Since the village was some miles away and we had no idea how long we would be, it was decided that Hannah would stay with Vivienne and David and I would take Jonathan and Julian. The day was hot and humid, which was hardly surprising. I wore a raspberry coloured silk shift dress which I'd worn with black high-heeled sandals for my sister's wedding - the outfit turned out to be somewhat inappropriate. The civil ceremony in town was straightforward, and very similar to an English registrar office wedding. It was after that the fun started.

We drove off into the bush in a convoy of cars, bumping along the rutted laterite roads, swerving to avoid erosions, bush dogs and heavily loaded bicycles. Usually the bicycles weren't ridden, but were used as a sort of wheelbarrow, steered gingerly along by their owners whilst huge bundles of plantain or sacks of charcoal, which were roped onto the saddle and frame, slithered dangerously from side to side.

Every now and then we would pass the wreckage of a burnt-out tank or plane, relics of the Biafran war, their rusted bodywork already disappearing beneath the luxuriant undergrowth of the encroaching forests. By now our clothes were sticking to our bodies, our faces covered in a fine film of sweat and laterite and our nostrils filled with the stench of diesel which belched out of passing trucks. But this was the Africa I loved and where I strangely felt completely at home.

Eventually we drew up outside a half- built two storey house. All over Africa you can see houses in various stages of completion. As the owners acquire some cash they build as much as they can afford. It may be a year or two before the next stage can be built, but crazy inflation and financial insecurity means that it's probably a good idea to do what they can when they can.

The building in front of us – I can't in all honesty call it a house – was made of grey breeze block. It had four walls, a roof and some internal block walls. Although the ceremony was to take place on the upper floor there were no stairs. Fortunately however there was a ladder. Now at the best of times I do not care for ladders. I especially do not like climbing ladders in a tight shift dress and high heels. But there was little option and I made it to the top with some pulling from the front, and some pushing from behind. The boys managed extremely well of course, and couldn't understand what the fuss was about.

Dotted around the room were a few metal chairs, lined up on the bare dusty floor. I pushed my way to the back and found myself alongside Ken, another ex-pat who was out for a few months. In the meantime the surrounding seats had been grabbed and I saw that David and the boys had been escorted to the front row.

The bride's father, dressed magnificently in national dress began the ceremony. A goat was dragged in together with a few bottles of gin. I hoped the goat would not have its throat cut in front of the boys. (Or me for that matter.)

The Chief began his welcome speech, saying how delighted he was that his daughter was marrying a white man. Ken leaned over to me and whispered 'Don't want to worry you Georgie, but have you noticed he keeps looking at David and not at Stan?' I had. I'd also noticed that David had noticed and that he kept turning to the boys, smiling and stroking their hair and trying at all cost to avoid eye contact with the Chief.

'I no ask £20 for my daughter', the chief intoned. 'I no asking £15 for my daughter. She marry white man, very good. I ask only £5.2s.6d.' What a bizarre number to choose, where had he seen it I wondered? However by this time he seemed to have sorted out the right White Man which was a relief to us all. The gin was opened and poured onto the floor, a libation to the gods. I licked my lips longingly. What I wouldn't have given for a long cold gin and tonic. Still, I suppose on this particular day the gods' needs were greater than mine.

A considerable time later we staggered down the ladder and the goat was dealt with behind a hut. We were served **Joliffe rice*** on chipped enamel plates with fried plantain. It was delicious and preferable to smoke salmon canapés, coronation chicken and the respectability of an English country wedding.

Some years later we met Stan and Esther in England with their small daughter. I wondered, silently, how Esther found life in rainy Manchester, far away from the vibrant life of her village home.

* * *

It was at the club that I'd first met Obi and her children. I'm ashamed to say that I can only remember the name of her small daughter, Inky. Imagine my delight when some months after our first meeting Obi had arrived at the house to ask if I'd like to help out at an important local ceremony. I had no idea what it might be but jumped at the chance of getting involved.

So a few days later we set off together in the car. I have to admit to feeling happy and quite light-headed that day. What a sense of relief at leaving the children and my responsibilities behind and having a few hours of grown-up independence.

We drove for ages through small villages busy with market stalls, swerving to miss the goats and stray bush dogs who wandered aimlessly across the pot-holed roads. At times all signs of human life disappeared as we cut through heavy rain forests whose thick luxuriant leaves offered welcome relief from the sun. I still had no idea where we were or where we were going. But as we bumped along I learnt from Obi that we had been chosen to assist in the lying in state of the late regional king. As an important chief's daughter Obi was considered to have a suitable pedigree for the job. Quite why I had been chosen was not at all clear. I could only think that it was because I was Obi's friend. But it was a unique privilege for a white woman to be allowed at the ceremony.

The car slowed down as we drew close the village. Although some of the houses were made of mud, several were constructed in more substantial brick and blocks. The entrance to the village was under newly erected temporary arches – two large vertical wooden poles with a horizontal pole joining them together. Several of these arches had been placed around the perimeter of the village and hanging from each one was a live chicken. Suspended upside down and tied by their feet to the pole they slowly rotated, squawking and flapping their way to death under the burning sun. This was not a good start.

We climbed out of the car and found ourselves in a huge area of trodden earth where the festival, dancing and singing would take place the following day. We were greeted warmly by two large and superbly colourful ladies who escorted us to the palace where the king's body was already lying in state. Our job I discovered was to decorate the bed so that his subjects' final view of him would be dignified and regal.

Now when I say palace I don't mean as in Buckingham or Blenheim. I mean as in two- story breeze block house. It was proof of great wealth. Inside, despite the open doors and windows, it was stifling. My heart was already pounding as we slowly climbed the stairs to the large bedroom. A six-month old corpse and temperatures in the upper nineties? I took a deep breath as we entered the room. Fortunately, one of his sons who was a Doctor had been able to store his body in a fridge.

The room was, by English standards, somewhat flamboyant. It was dominated by a huge shiny four-poster brass bed much loved by Nigerians and available at all roadside furniture stalls. I glanced down to see the wizened figure of a little old man. His ears and nostrils were stuffed with cotton wool. Everyone looked eagerly at me. What did I think? I scrabbled round my brain for some suitable words. 'He must have been a very interesting man'. They nodded and smiled appreciatively. I breathed a sigh of relief. So far, so good.

Then the two large ladies produced rolls of net curtaining and bunches of plastic roses they used to give away in the 60's with washing powder. It was clearly not my place to make creative suggestions and I dutifully did as I was told. Homes and Gardens, this was not.

Sometime later, we stepped back to admire our handy-work. The four-poster was now festooned with swathes of nylon netting, gathered at the four corners with bunches of red plastic roses.

As we left the room (none too soon for my taste) they told me that until recently (probably 50 or 60 years previously) when a king died he was not allowed to go into the afterlife alone, so his subjects raided neighbouring villages where they took prisoners who were buried alive with him. For a moment I felt a slight wave of panic – then I saw them smiling and they reassured me that I really had no need to worry for the practice had now died out. I wonder…?

The following day I returned, this time with the children and David. It was a wonderful send-off for the old King. Music, dancing, laughter and plenty of food. The air was filled with dust as a thousand feet stamped the earth to the intoxicating rhythm of drums. Exotic feathers, vibrant costumes and giant-sized coral and ivory jewellery set off the swaying glistening bodies of his subjects. This was the Africa I had come to see.

*   *   *

The festivities over, our day to day life continued in a new found rhythm of its own. I tried as much as possible to vary it for the children, to keep them amused and stimulated. Of course we had no such diversions as television, computers or even a telephone. So we had to rely upon trips into town, to the markets, to the swimming pool. David took it upon himself to run the pool at the club, importing all the necessary chemicals. In fact he rather over-did the copper sulphate and slowly our children's beautiful blonde hair turned green.

One day I asked David if he could send the car back after he reached the factory, as I needed to go to the market. The children were delighted to be let off studies and we all piled in with our baskets and headed down-town. The roads were a nightmare – full of holes and jammed with old carts, rusting cars and bikes and herds of goats meandering in and out of the traffic.

Suddenly Moses our driver swerved off the road to avoid an obstacle. We all looked out. A body of a young man lay face down on what remained of the tarmac. A knife stuck out from his shoulder blades, and a pool of dark blood which had already dried was swarming with flies. I tried to persuade the children to close their eyes or look the other way. But what child in his right mind is going to be interested in vegetable stalls when he can look at a dead body?

'Why aren't the police here?' I asked Moses. 'Shouldn't they be removing the body or looking for clues?' Moses glanced at me through the driving mirror, shrugged his shoulders. 'These things happen' he said indifferently. I could see him wondering what all the fuss was about.

But not to be deterred, I decided that we should report the matter immediately, so we headed off to the police station. How young and innocent I was. At that time 'the station' was a small hut with a metal roof. One policeman, the only policeman I think, sat outside under the shade of a tree. He was leaning back balancing on the back legs of his chair and picking his nails with a small of stick. I explained that there was a body lying in the main street. Yes, he knew about it. In fact he'd informed the C.I.D and they'd said they might come today or they might come tomorrow. He was very charming and friendly but he'd done all he could. End of story.

We left, my duty done and set off in search of tomatoes and bananas taking the long way round and making sure we avoided the body.

8

THE MARKETS

I do not like shopping. In fact I'd go so far as to say I hate shopping. Wandering aimlessly around crowded shops fills me with dread. But there are however, two exceptions. Shopping for books and shopping for food. And shopping for food in Africa was a delicious adventure.

As a small child I had been taken to the weekly town market every Wednesday by my grandmother. To me it had been like finding myself in the middle of a wonderful theatre – the cries of the stallholders, the colours of the fruit and vegetables, the smell of cheeses and above all the taste of the Italian ice-cream which was my weekly treat. I can still see so clearly the red and white van where I queued with my sixpence clutched tightly in my fist, and taste the creamy richness of the swirling ice-cream mountain. In post war England what a luxury that had been.

Arriving for the first time in Nigeria I wasn't sure where to start when it came to food shopping. What would I find and how was I going to adapt our diet to what was available locally? There was a supermarket of sorts in the town, managed by Denis a charming and friendly Ibo, who was very proud of his one and only freezer. The only problem was that he didn't understand the concept of frozen food, or the fact that freezers needed to be colder than fridges or that they couldn't cope with frequent power cuts. On my first visit he steered me proudly in the direction of the freezer and pointed out the piles of carefully packed sausages. They were green and soft to the touch. 'These are not good, Denis' I tried to explain to him. 'They have to be hard, like rocks. The freezer needs to be much colder – it's not working properly and if people eat the sausage they will be ill'. Needless to say his freezer never worked.

He looked very disappointed, then his eyes lit up 'Don't worry madame, I will send to London immediately for an engineer!' But he was a generous and willing source of local information and one day took us all to visit the erosions – an extraordinary lunar-like landscape, where the rains had washed away most of the ground but left thin needle sharp towers, on which were perched small rocks or pebbles. The towers stood several feet tall and stretched as far as the eye could see.

There were of course stalls of meat available in the open market, but the meat was so fly-blown and there was no way of telling how old it was or how long it had been sitting under the blistering sun. Buying it was not a risk I felt I could take.

Then one morning someone told me that some Hausa – those tall, aristocratic Nigerians from the north of the country – were driving their cattle down from the arid towns of Kano and Kaduna and would stop outside Onitsha to sell fresh meat. Leaving the children behind with Rose our new help, I grabbed the car and the driver – wives were not allowed to drive company cars in those days – and headed out of town.

Hundreds of long-horned cattle, emaciated by their arduous journey south, whirled across the road and dusty roadsides, foraging for every bit of grass they could find. Their owners had set up wobbly wooden stalls and their great cleavers, spattered with blood, glittered in the dazzling heat. Everywhere there was the stench of death and of warm coagulated blood. Millions of flies swarmed around us and hundreds of vultures scavenged on the mountains of intestines and half-formed foetuses which steamed as they were ripped from torn bellies. This meat couldn't have been much 'fresher'.

It was a picture from hell. Had I been faced with such a sight back home no doubt I would have been horrified. But somehow there I was able to accept it – this was a different life, raw and basic and I needed to feed my family.

The meat had been hacked into lumps and I had to make a guess as to what I was buying. Everything seemed to be the same price and since there were no scales I had to try and judge the weight and then bargain. There were no other white women there and the Hausa were bemused to see me. But they were friendly enough, if a little disdainful. I was after all a mere woman. I filled my enamel bucket with tough looking meat and headed home.

Back in my kitchen I set about trying to work out just what I'd bought. I discovered to my delight, a large piece of fillet which I carefully extracted and put in my tiny freezer compartment. Such luxury and so cheap. The rest was kept for stewing – very long and slow stewing. But it was fresh and it was meat and fortunately we all had good strong teeth.

Some weeks later much of my treasured fillet was used to feed a small owl which a passing traveller came to sell me. It had clearly been stolen from a nest and he knew only too well how gullible the Europeans were when it came to small birds and animals. But, knowing that he too needed to eat, I bought the owl from him and I fed it daily on my precious fillet steak until it was old enough and strong enough to let go. However before that day arrived the owl mysteriously disappeared. No doubt it was in someone's cooking pot, probably the nightwatchman's. When you're hungry any sort of protein, feathered or furred will do.

One morning I'd heard great shouting and rushed outside. At the bottom of the garden I saw a group of excited boys throwing stones up into a tree. I went over and asked them what they were after. 'Wild animal, up in tree. Kill it, kill it.'

My protests went unheeded of course so I asked them if and when they did destroy the poor animal would they bring it to show me. I was intrigued as nearly all wild life in that part of Nigeria had been slaughtered many years ago, and I couldn't imagine what it could be. Half an hour later a group of boys marched up to the front door calling 'Madame, madame, come see!' I went out and saw a large dead ginger tom being held up by its tail. Lunch for their family that day.

The next time I went to the Hausa market I took my kitchen scales with me, much to everyone's amusement. But at least it made it easier to work out a price acceptable to us all. Unfortunately I don't remember ever finding another large piece of fillet again.

Fruit and vegetables were much easier to find. I had simply to drive down to the open market which stretched along the banks of the river and pick my way carefully around the piles of rubbish deciding which stalls had the freshest and most appetizing goods. It took some time to get used to the mis-shapen vegetables and fruit. The tomatoes looked extraordinary – bizarre and monstrous - but alright for cooking. Everything I bought had to be soaked in Milton disinfectant, as all the vegetables were watered from the river or local streams into which the sewage flowed. The secret was to cook with strong herbs and spices. Unfortunately Milton flavoured salads were distinctly unpleasant so we didn't eat them too often. However we all loved **roasted vegetables***.

At first we often had stomach upsets but nothing too disastrous and in the end we seemed to build up an immunity to the local bacteria. Although I recall with horror one time when we were all ill and had no electricity for three days, so therefore no water because it had to be pumped up to the tank in the roof. We were forced to fill up buckets from a standpipe and refill the cisterns by hand. I seemed to spend hours filling up containers and swabbing the bathrooms with disinfectant. How easy my life seems now.

Our breakfast every morning consisted of freshly squeezed oranges – the skin of African oranges is green not orange – bananas, paw-paw and mangoes. Occasionally the children begged for cornflakes and sometimes I could find them in the local shop but at an enormous price and sometimes stale. So they were a rare treat. The local bread was awful, very sweet with the texture of cotton wool. The only time we found good bread in W. Africa was on a visit to Côte d'Ivoire where we were able to buy true French baguettes and croissants.

Fortunately we all loved fish and the Niger perch was plentiful, tasty and quite cheap. I remember a great evening when we were entertaining some of the local community and had decided to serve fish and chips, English style. Raphael was bemused as we made the **batter*** together and I discussed how we were going to serve the meal out of newspapers, lined with greaseproof paper. I could see him look at me with shock and amazement. Having been raised by English missionaries he was very proper, utterly charming, honest, reliable and quite used to English eccentricities. But he had never in his life, been asked to serve a meal out of newspaper. We ate a great deal of fish in those days as it was always plentiful. However we had little choice – Niger Perch or Niger Perch. But it was delicious, lightly battered, curried or served with hollandaise sauce.

* * *

I may have surprised Raphael with some of my ideas but on the other hand he was equally capable of shocking me. Every morning he used to bring me a cup of tea before we started preparing breakfast. One morning I took a much needed mouthful and spat it out immediately. It was awful. I went into the kitchen to ask him what he'd done. He smiled proudly at me. 'Ah, madame, I thought I give you nice treat. Today I boil the tea-leaves in a saucepan milk to make it special for you'. I thanked him but thought maybe we should stick to the old way of pouring on boiling water.

Occasionally David would come home and tell me that we were expecting visitors from London the following week. My feelings would be mixed. It would be great to meet some new faces and have the opportunity to entertain. They might even bring me a book or two. But on the other hand I would have to organize a dinner party and that would take some planning. So much would depend on what food was available locally. If the Hausas weren't driving down cattle, meat would be difficult. Our nearest big town was Enugu, some seventy miles away. There they had a large supermarket, so a few days before our guests were due I would decide on two or three menus, to prepare for all eventualities and availabilities, write out the shopping list for each and then arrange for the driver to take me shopping.

It would be a long day as in those days the roads were poor and potholed. (Twenty-five years later we sped easily along dual-carriageways.) We would set out after breakfast and by lunch time arrive at the supermarket. The first time I went I remember how eagerly I rushed inside, full of expectation. What a shock I'd had when I saw row upon row of empty shelves. The only available goods were small tins of tomato puree and tinned anchovies. My carefully thought out menus were completely useless. It was then I realized that I had to start from a different place. Find the ingredients first then make up my own recipes. Fortunately I loved cooking so we usually managed to eat reasonably well. If **we** tired of avocadoes, fresh fish, fruit salad and **chocolate mousse,*** our visitors seemed to consider them delightful treats.

* * *

Our time in Onitsha was full of ups and downs. Some days I felt on a high, loving every moment of the heat and sun, the romance of African life. At other times I wept with frustration and despair. David worked such long hours and keeping the children amused all day and every day was often difficult and stressful. But slowly I became part of the local community, which to be honest was much more enjoyable than the ex-pat community.

I'd been delighted to be asked to be the Lady Member of the Social Club. This meant that I was allowed to approve or veto new members who'd applied to join, and also that I was to supervise the running of the kitchens.

So guns blazing, I made my first visit to inspect the kitchens. I was not impressed. The surfaces and walls were thick with grease. Metaphorically rolling up my sleeves, I poured a bowl of hot water and demonstrated to the staff how we were going to clean the worktops, scrub down the walls and floors. They looked at me with disdain. 'But madame, what is the point,' the chief steward asked 'they will only get dirty again.'

At my first committee meeting they were discussing possible new members. I admitted that I didn't know the person they were discussing. 'Yes, of course you do' the chairman said. 'He's the black man.' I looked around the table. They were all Nigerian and to me, all black. But then I realized what they meant. There were so many shades of skin colour ranging from various shades of brown, to reddish hues and blue-black. When they said 'black man' that's just what they meant, a man with a truly dark black complexion.

In the end though the majority decided to 'black ball him.' I could hardly stop myself from bursting out laughing. I don't think they'd seen the joke.

Then, suddenly, one day it was time to return to the UK for our leave. But as we packed our suitcases for our six week break in England stopping en route in Naples and Paris, I little knew that I would not return to Onitsha for another twenty-five years .

Back in England David would be told that he was being moved to Ghana, this time as Managing Director of two textile mills which needed rescuing.

So there was no time to say goodbye to Raphael, to Obi and Dada. No time to pack up our belongings or make a sentimental journey down the great River Niger.

What did I feel? A mixture of sadness and relief. Sadness to be leaving a fascinating world which was so alien to anything I had ever known, and yet part relief that we would be moving to Accra, a metropolitan city with schools, shops and hopefully the chance to widen my horizons yet again.

This ability to move in and out of another culture, to exchange experiences and traditions, is what has been so rewarding throughout my life. Even now, years later, those Nigerian memories burn as bright as ever, warming the coldest winter days.

9

THE GOLD COAST

At our first meeting David had talked about his life on the coast. Being young and ignorant and keen not to appear stupid, I daren't ask him which coast it was. East coast, south coast; Bridlington or Bournemouth?

It was only when he started to talk about Africa that I realised he meant 'The Gold Coast', otherwise known as Ghana. He'd gone out at the age of twenty –one to run a business selling African prints, was based in Kumasi and spent the next ten years travelling between and working in both Ghana and Nigeria.

Now years later we were all unexpectedly being transferred to Accra for another tour of duty. The problem was that all our personal belongings were in Onitsha awaiting our return And so a few weeks later we landed at Accra airport with only the suitcases we'd taken on holiday but with the addition of new sets of clothes and a few more books and toys.

It was some weeks before David had the time to sort out a van and driver and set off by road back to Eastern Nigeria to collect our belongings. It was a very long and arduous journey passing through two other countries, Togo and Benin State. But at least he had the opportunity to say goodbye to everyone, and with Raphael's help emptied all the drawers and cupboards, took pictures off the walls, unplugged the lamps and crated them all for the bumpy journey back to our new home. Sadly my butterfly collection which I had carefully pinned on boards to dry before mounting them, had been eaten by ants and only a few remained intact.

With him I'd sent letters of goodbye and thanks to Raphael and Vivienne and Rose, to Obi and Dada and to our Nigerian and English colleagues with whom we'd shared fascinating and frustrating times. But it was sad for me not to be able to see them all for the last time.

When we returned to Onitsha, more than twenty-five years later, most of our colleagues had disappeared but a handful still remained and they'd arranged a delightful lunch for us in the factory. We were even invited to our old home which then housed the Nigerian factory manager. How small it seemed all those years later and yet how vividly I could still see the ghosts of our three blonde children running and laughing through the rooms.

However it was the garden which had changed the most. Those tiny shrubs and trees we'd planted were now huge trees, their luxuriant green leaves turning the garden into a small forest. David and I set off to retrace the past, strolling through the garden, recalling plant names, the bullets and grenades. We had to persuade the 'entourage' not to join us. We just felt the need to recapture those magical times when we were young and full of hope with our whole lives before us.

* * *

Now here we were in the centre of Accra, capital of Ghana, living in an old colonial house whose huge compound was filled with guava and mango trees which sheltered us from the busy main road running past the house. The two-storey white-washed house had a pillared porch and terrace, a huge living and dining room with high ceilings, parquet floors and two walls of French windows. Upstairs were three bedrooms, a dressing room and two bathrooms. Our bedroom opened out onto a verandah from where I could watch the children race around the termite hills, free from the danger of bullets and rogue soldiers.

And luxury of luxuries, it was only a ten minute drive to the markets and shops where I could buy much more than I ever could in Onitsha. But there were still desperate shortages and soap powder would arrive one day then never be seen for the next three months. There were supermarkets of a sort, modern hotels, skyscraper office blocks, Lebanese restaurants, countless churches and numerous Embassies and High Commissions. Shirley Temple Black, the American Ambassador lived a few doors away but in a much smarter and larger house heavily guarded by Marines.

But despite the trappings of twentieth-century progress and the superficial veneer of cosmopolitan chic, the open storm-drains were still filled with stinking rubbish, the roadsides were awash with piles of plastic litter and rusting tins. In the shadow of the air-conditioned supermarkets rickety stalls offered bulbous tomatoes and wilting lettuces. The traffic was appalling and the air often filled with stifling diesel fumes. Whilst we were there the traffic rules were changed and we suddenly had to start driving on the right and not the left. Can you image the chaos? But despite it all the city was heaven in comparison to Lagos. People were friendly and laid-back and I always remember it as a city of laughter.

* * *

We'd only been there a few weeks when disaster struck. I was rushed into a clinic for an emergency operation leaving the children with a new nanny while David was up to his eyes in his new job. The clinic, run by a delightful Dr Kwako (such an unfortunate name for a Doctor) was modern and streamlined. But like most things in Africa there was always something to spoil the overall effect.

In this case it was the nurse entering my room on the morning of the operation saying 'Walk!' I had to get out of bed, put the sheet around my shoulders and walk across the dusty lawn to the operating room trailing the sheet behind me and disturbing comatose insects who sprang angrily to life.   The theatre was modern and very up to date, but it didn't feel quite right hopping on to the operating table and kicking my dirty sandals underneath whilst the nurse threw my dusty sheet onto the floor.

As I lay there heart beating I watched a few kamikaze flies buzz around the room and came to the grim conclusion that this was probably the last ceiling I would ever see. When I discovered the surgeon was also the anaesthetist I almost got off the table. What would become of my motherless children?

But I survived and the operation was a success. After a few days I went home and resting one morning on my bed while the children played outside I suddenly heard a great commotion.

'Mummy, mummy quick, look what I've done. I've fallen out of the guava tree.' Jonathan rushed into my room, holding out his arm – it didn't take a trained doctor to realise that it was broken. His arm hung at a right angle between his elbow and his hand. I laid him on the bed and 'phoned the office.

After several attempts I got through to the factory where David was in the middle of a board meeting. He arrived half an hour later and we put Jonathan into the car and headed to the Military Hospital as the company Doctor had advised.

There was a huge military camp just outside the city, on the way to the Airport. There he was seen by a splendid Major Day who set his arm whilst they found a bed for me too. What a traumatic week. Looking back I often wondered how I didn't take the next plane home. Years later when we returned we heard that the charming Major had become a Brigadier, which didn't surprise us at all.

* * *

Once again David was heavily involved in his job and it was up to me to sort out the rest of our lives. At the top of my list was finding a school for the boys and a nursery school for Hannah. During their time in Nigeria their formal education had been hit and miss – mostly miss - but apart from catching up academically they also needed to mix with other children and learn to socialise once again.

There was an excellent International School which unfortunately was full but eventually we found a place for the boys at the renowned Christ The King school which was attached to the Catholic Church and which then still employed Austrian nuns. Neither David nor I had any religious inclinations but David had been taught by the Irish Christian Brothers whom he'd liked very much and who'd managed to instil in him a love of learning if not religion.

There were very few European children in the school but I think it was a very valuable lesson for Jonathan and Julian to discover what it was like to be "different." A local seamstress ran up their uniform of maroon shorts and shirts and they soon settled into the daily routine of morning school. They started at 8.00 a.m and finished at lunchtime. The afternoons were far too hot for anyone to concentrate.

After a couple of months there Jonathan returned home clearly upset. His teacher, one of the nuns, had told him that because he had not been baptised (none of our children were) he could not go to heaven. As a lapsed Catholic myself the comment merely reinforced my negative views of the church. However it clearly was a problem for Jonathan and so we agreed that he could be baptised. A few weeks later there was a big ceremony in the Cathedral led by the Bishop and he was embraced by the Catholic faith. Needless to say his faith didn't last long. But he felt happier for the rest of his time at school. Twenty-five years later he was to marry in a Catholic church and had to produce his baptismal certificate.

Of course we'd never bothered to collect it and as far as we knew it was still somewhere in the archives of Christ the King Church in Ghana. I contacted a friend who was then living in Accra and asked her if she could enquire at the church. A few weeks later his baptismal certificate arrived in the post, much to our astonishment.

Not far from our house I discovered a kindergarten run by Nora Sakwe-Mante, an English nurse who had settled in Ghana during its colonial days, becoming a hospital sister and marrying a local Doctor. So each morning I took Hannah to the school where she mixed with local and ex-pat children and became firm friends with Elena a Greek-

American girl whose parents Andreas and Louise became our closest friends and with whom we would spend many happy weekends on the beach.

Sadly Louise had been born with a faulty heart and tired very easily. But she was a great needlewoman and cook and whenever we went over to play bridge (not seriously) she would make us her **Brownies*** to eat with coffee. Five years after leaving Ghana we stood in Putney cemetery one cold March day, whilst they buried Louise.

* * *

Now suddenly I had time on my hands – four hours of freedom each morning. How to fill it?

Each Friday morning the local "stitch and bitch" club was held at the British High Commissioner's house. It was a good way to meet people and the High Commissioner's wife Mrs S, was delightfully English and slightly eccentric. Patchwork seemed to be the preferred activity and the ladies were all very industrious and produced some beautiful work. I on the other hand was completely useless and not really interested in sewing or knitting, but I enjoyed my mornings there, if only to listen and observe.

The social pecking order was wondrous to behold. High Commission staff didn't really like mixing with 'trade' or 'commercial'. The fact that we made the money and they spent it was beside the point. Whilst the rest of us struggled to find luxuries in the local shops, they had all the goodies imported for their use only.

During my first morning there one lady was digging to find out what exactly David did. This would reveal whether I was suitable for the cocktail list or not. I explained where he worked. 'Yes, but what actually does he DO?' I prevaricated. She pushed even further. 'Well,' I replied, 'he's the Managing. Director.' Her face broke into a huge smile. 'Oh, but you must come to dinner' she gushed. Needless to say I made sure we didn't.

But I loved the elegance of the High Commissioner's house, the grand piano with its signed photograph of the Queen in its silver frame; the attentive stewards in their sparkling white uniforms; the delicate china and silver teapots; the lush weed-free sweeping lawns and vibrant oleanders and canna lilies. Occasionally you would bump into a visiting dignitary waiting on the steps for the limo to whisk them away. Lord Denning - one of the most illustrious judges of the twentieth century - and his wife were delightful and friendly as we met one morning on the front steps and chatted as if we were old friends. I was amused one Friday when Mrs S. told us that next week's meeting would have to be cancelled as they were entertaining Joan Lester, a minister from London. 'Unless, of course', Mrs S said 'anyone would want to meet her?' The raised eyebrow and slightly quizzical smile, indicted that she thought we probably wouldn't.

But one morning a week in the splendours of the High Commissioner's house was amusing but not quite enough to stretch the brain. I decided that I needed to do something to stop my brain atrophying and decided that maybe I needed to fill in the gaps in my education. As I said before maths, physics, chemistry were subjects I'd found perplexing. So I thought that maybe I should try to improve my maths and perhaps tackle the physics as well. Without a laboratory the chemistry was out of the question. But where to find a teacher?

Asking around it became clear that I should head out to the university and make enquiries there. So one morning I borrowed the car and set off to knock on a few doors on the campus. In the end I managed to find a young English woman Thelma D, a nuclear physicist married to a Ghanaian physicist, but who was still not full employed and clearly could do with the money.

So twice a week she came to our house where she worked hard at trying to switch my brain on. I really enjoyed the lessons and I think she enjoyed the lunches. Living off Ghanaian wages was really difficult when you'd been brought up in Western Europe with all the luxuries we took for granted. Today I wonder what became of her and if her marriage survived? So many mixed marriages fell apart, especially where the wife was European. The standards of living in Africa were often dramatically lower and the role and expectations of a wife were very different.

As I sorted out my papers to come to France I came across all my old maths and physics workbooks. I was astounded to see what I'd been able to do. I couldn't remember a single word of any of it and had retained absolutely nothing. Ah well, at least I tried.

* * *

My most lasting memories of Ghana are the weekends we spent by the beach. With the job came the use of a small motor boat, a canoe and a small hut in Adda on the banks of the river Volta. A short journey by boat led us to a wonderful sandy beach from where we could swim safely and easily, sheltered from the thundering seas by a long reef.

On a Sunday morning we'd pack up the cold bag filling it with chicken, meat and fish for the barbeque, salads and fruit. The boot would be packed with crates of beer and soft drinks, a medical chest, sun lotions, sun hats, arm bands and spare fuel. It was nearly as complicated as moving house but after a few weeks we got it down to a fine art.

Then soon after breakfast we'd head out leaving the city behind, the children already hyped up with excitement at the thought of running wild on the beach. It took us about two hours and we'd usually stop somewhere in a small village to buy a bunch of bananas and a pineapple from a wayside stall. We always sent a message ahead to Joseph who lived in Adda and whose job it was to maintain the boat and the cabin and also to drive the boat down to the beach. When we arrived he'd already lit the barbeque and swept out the cabin which was usually full of dust and sand. The cabin was in fact an old caravan which had a mosquito proof room built on to it. It was not pretty but it was wonderful.

The river was quite wide at this point, and the banks were heavily shaded with lush dark green vegetation. Turquoise and scarlet and black and white kingfishers darted brilliantly from tree to river diving expertly for lunch whilst huge moniter lizards occasionally emerged from the undergrowth and ambled along the banks.

David would take the boys canoeing whilst I sorted out lunch and Hannah played in the shade of the trees. The pudding would be David's responsibility on those occasions and his favourite was **bananas cooked in butter, sugar, rum and orange juice***.

Then we would all set off for the beach in the motor launch – how we loved the fast ride, the wind blowing away all our cares. Minutes later we'd reach the lovely shallow bay which we always had to ourselves. Switching off the engine Joseph would drift as near as he could to the shore and out we would jump into the knee- high warm water and paddle onto the white hot beach.

Beyond the reef the Atlantic Ocean roared angrily, but we were safe swimming in our turquoise and white paradise. The beaches were littered with wonderful shells, mosly broken but occasionally we'd find some perfect specimens which I still have today. Each time I pick one up the years slip away and I return to that perfect peace.

Returning twenty-five years later we discovered that Adda had become a smart resort with a busy yacht club, elegant holiday homes and luxurious Mercedes parked beneath the palms. But surprisingly I felt little sadness or regret– it was just a different place, a different time and I was a different person.

*   *   *

However life in Ghana was not always so stress free. At that time the military government was led by Colonel Acheamphong who had seized power in a *coup d'etat* two years before we arrived. Promoting himself to General he led a government which was steeped in corruption but at the same time he implemented the change to the metric system of measurement, the right-hand drive and the Operation Feed Yourself programme. But as in most African countries there was always the rumbling of discontent, the jostlings for power.

Rumours of another coup were rife during our stay, and Stephen and Regina, our steward and nanny usually kept me up-to-date with the latest gossip.

One evening David had to take a visitor from London back to the airport which lay some miles out of town past the huge military camp. As night fell the air was suddenly filled with loud explosions. Regina came running into the sitting room. 'Madame, madame, the coup is happening.' Stephen rushed in after her together with the night watchman a magnificent 6'5 Hausa man, complete with cross-bow. They were clearly panicked.

My heart sank – there was no way David was going to get home. They'd close the airport, block off the roads and soldiers would be roaming around shooting everything that moved. Gathering the children together I grabbed our passports, money and valuables and then rang Andreas and Louise who lived not too far away. 'Don't worry' Andreas said, 'I'll drive round and collect you all now. Leave a note for David in case he gets back'.

Twenty minutes later we were in their house drinking a stiff whisky listening to the explosions and worrying about David. An anxious hour passed before we heard the crunch of gravel as a car drew up. Out stepped David looking calm and relaxed.

I rushed out. 'Are you ok? How did you get through? Who's leading the coup?"'

'What coup?' he asked looking somewhat perplexed.

'The gunfire, the explosions!' I said.

He burst out laughing, 'There's a big celebration somewhere outside town – a great firework display!'

So we all had another drink, this time to celebrate and then made our way home to reassure Stephen and Regina.

In fact General Acheamphong lasted another three years before the revolution which brought Fl. Lt . Jerry Rawlings to power. The General was executed by firing squad in June 1979.

*   *   *

The general unrest spread to the workers at the factories and one night as we finished dinner David received a message to say that the factory was surrounded by militant workers who were picketing the gates and creating mayhem. Naturally I didn't want him to go as I knew how easily these things could get out of hand. But of course quite rightly, he set off to try and sort things out. It was a long evening whilst I waited for his return, worrying that something dreadful may have happened. If only we'd had mobile phones in those days. But eventually he arrived safely - although shaken. It had not been a pleasant evening. On seeing his car arrive the workers surrounded it rocking it violently from side to side whilst the driver tried to edge his way through the gates. They'd even broken in and filled the offices with graffitti, although they'd kindly covered the walls first with paper rather than write on the walls!

*   *   *

David was an only child and so it was difficult for his parents to be without him and their grandchildren for such a long time. In those days we had no computers, emails, or mobiles. Telephoning was difficult enough in Ghana, international calls were a nightmare and could take hours to book in advance and then we'd be cut off. So we decided that we'd bring John and Edith out to join us for a month.

At that time were in their 70s and had rarely travelled outside England. They were thrilled at the chance to travel all the way to Africa but understandably were nervous. We knew the Swissair representative in Accra and with his help we organized a trip which they were to relish for the rest of their lives. He arranged for them to have a personal escort, to stay overnight in Zurich on the way out and then in Geneva on the way back. They were looked after like royalty.

The climate in West Africa is ideally suited to older people and children. John always felt the cold and was usually huddled up in a heavy coat. In Ghana he was in heaven – luxuriating in the humidity and heat. He swam at Adda in his underpants, strolled along the beach in his straw hat and felt completely at home. Edith couldn't get over having 'servants' and loved sitting on the stoop in a wicker chair, drinking iced-tea and supervising the garden boys.

One Saturday lunchtime we were all invited to the house of an English girl I'd met, who was married to a Ghanaian whose family had been prominent politicians in the past. They'd met and married in England and now they lived permanently in Accra with their three children and not very much money.

The house was a very basic concrete bungalow with a yard but no garden. As we drew up we saw a large Ghanaian lady standing in the mid-day sun pounding cassava with a huge wooden pestle and mortar. As she leaned over the bowl the sweat dripped from her forehead onto the cassava. This was to be our lunch.

My heart sank – Edith was a very proper English lady and I realized very soon that lunch was to be a real problem. The chewy meat stew arrived, hot with pepper sauce, together with a huge bowl of fou-fou - the cooked cassava which now resembled a bowl of uncooked bread dough. There were no knives or forks and we had to tear off the fou-fou with our fingers and dip it into the sauce and meat. It seemed a very long hot lunch and although our hosts were charming we were all glad to say goodbye. As we drove away in our air-conditioned car I thought how difficult the lives of so many European wives married to African men were – their expectations were sadly so very different from the realities. Mixed marriages in the UK seemed to work much better.

Life in Ghana was not without humour, which was just as well. One day the driver arrived at the house with a delivery from David. As the phone wasn't working and I needed to discuss something urgently with him, I asked Amos to take me back to the factory. He was very reluctant and tried to put me off. I couldn't understand it.

In the end I insisted as it was important. So grumbling he agreed and we set off. Then he said 'I have to pick up Mr A to take him back to the office.

Now Mr A, the Ghanaian Personnel Manager had the reputation of being a ladies man with interesting interviewing techniques. 'Fine' I replied. 'That's not a problem.' But it clearly was.

After a few minutes on the main road we turned off unexpectedly. As we bumped along the uneven road I assumed we must be going to his home. We turned up at a ramshackle two storey house with large upstairs veranda. Hanging over the balustrade were a number of 'ladies' whose profession was unmistakable. We'd arrived at a local brothel. Now I knew why Amos was so reluctant to take me with him!

Finding a yellowing old newspaper on the back seat I concentrated on reading the headlines whilst the ladies smiled and waved at me. Amos returned after a few minutes later saying that Mr A wasn't there. What a surprise! He must have been hiding until I'd gone and would have to find his own way home.

I decided to say nothing to David, which was probably wise.

*   *   *

There are so many happy memories of our time in Ghana. The weekend trips to Aburi Gardens, a peaceful botanical garden some 39 km from Accra where the most exotic plants and exquisite orchids were to be found. In the grounds lay the wreck of an old helicopter which became a playground for the children. There too we saw the enormous, sacred silk cotton tree, one of the largest trees in W Africa., growing to a girth of 7 metres. Once the hills had been forested with them but now only one remained and who knows for how long. The fluffy kapok it produced was used as a substitute for cotton wool, its seeds were pounded and used in a soup or roasted whole. Its white wood was used for making furniture, including coffins.

Often we would take a picnic with us, stopping en route at the wayside vegetable stalls to buy bananas and mangoes. But in the end the picnics became impossible as we were soon surrounded by children anxious to join in. There was never enough food to go around!

As in Nigeria, the local markets were fascinating and colourful. Two or three times a week I would make my way downtown, wandering among the stalls, looking for fresh fruit and vegetables. One day I took Hannah with me – she was two at the time – but she suddenly missed her footing and fell down into a storm drain which was full of stinking rotting wet rubbish. I grabbed her quickly and was suddenly surrounded by the ladies of the market who appeared with clean clothes, shoes and water to clean her. So we stripped her off and with much cooing and laughing the stall-holders helped clean her up, and we returned home with her wet clothes in a plastic sack and a depleted purse.

The next time that I caused them such amusement was when the driver dropped me off in the middle of the huge market to wander around on my own. I'd just filled my basket with vegetables and fruit when a local man suddenly grabbed hold of me proclaiming 'You have gone straight to my heart, I will take you for my wife.' Shrieks of laughter came from the brightly clad and turbaned stallholders and I managed to release myself with the feeble excuse that I already had a husband.

In addition to all the wonderful fruit and vegetables, one of the culinary joys of living in Ghana was that we could get hold of fresh fish direct from the beaches and on Saturday afternoons we would head for the port of Tema where we could buy fresh crayfish straight from the fishermen. We'd pile them into our enamel bucket and head home to cook them for dinner. Unless we were entertaining I preferred to cook myself at the weekends and a favourite Saturday dinner would be **avocadoes, prawns and mayonnaise**,* or **crayfish with lime and coriander dressing.***

* * *

Sometimes though our excursions were tinged with sadness. Driving west along the coast we once spent a wonderful day, discovering bustling villages and townships, walking along the beach savouring the warmth of the sun, the brilliance of the blue skies and white sand. But our destination was Elmina Castle whose infamous history turned the blood cold. Built in 1472 by the Portuguese as a trading post – it was known then as 'A Mina' because of the gold which was mined there. But then an equally rewarding business grew up. It soon became the centre of the Atlantic slave trade. The castle acted as a depot where the slaves were kept in the most appalling conditions and those who survived their stay soon left from the castle's infamous 'Door of No Return' and headed for the new Portuguese colonies.

Our children were undoubtedly too young to fully appreciate the horror of those times. But as I sit at my desk now looking at a photograph David took then of our blonde happy children sitting on the beach with the Castle on the far horizon, I realize again, what fortunate lives we have all had. Our children's lives still full of promise, our own lives truly fulfilled.

* * *

David's work continued to be consuming and involved a great deal of travel away from home. But before long we had big decision to make. Did David opt for a career in Africa or did we go back to England? Certainly the temptations of life as an expatriate were great but there was one enormous drawback. Sooner or later the children would have to return to England for their education. But I had seen too many tearful children and distraught parents at the airport and I knew that I could never send them away whilst they were still so young.

And so eventually we decided to return to England and a home posting. David continued to travel to and from Africa and oversee African businesses until his retirement. I was lucky enough, especially in the later years to travel extensively with him. What a joy it has been to see so much of that exotic yet tortured continent, to see places rarely visited by European tourists.

Looking back I sometimes ask myself which I preferred – my time in Nigeria or Ghana? I think it must be Nigeria, not just because it was my first experience of Africa but because it was so very different. I lived a life there which was often tough and lonely but which was enormously challenging. Life in Ghana was certainly easier, more relaxed, more cosmopolitan but for me it lacked the challenges which I so love.

Many years later we returned with the children – who were then grown up – to Africa. But this time to the east. It was after my car accident and I wanted to say thank you to them all for helping me through the dark and difficult days. They were all still single and so were free to take two weeks and travel with us. It was a wonderful trip. We took the train from Nairobi to Mombasa, an exciting thirteen hour journey overnight, in a rather dilapidated train where dinner was served by delightful stewards in holey gloves and frayed jackets.

At the Tamarind restaurant we sat on the terrace overlooking the moonlit Mombasa lagoon drinking dawas, the local heady concoction of vodka, crushed ice, lime juice and honey. The cries of the muezzin calling the faithful to prayer filled the night air, as we worked our way through a mouth-watering menu.

Julian started with a huge plate of sushi followed by peppered steak, Jonathan and Hannah had stuffed calamari whilst David and I had Indian prawns with lime and coriander dressing, served with slices of fanned avocado. For our main course David had hot and sour fish and prawns, I had seafood salad with mango, avocado and pawpaw, whilst Hannah worked her way through a 600gm lobster.

Two days later we drove into Tanzania, through Moshe and Arusha, glimpsing Mount Kilimanjaro through the clouds and then wound our way up to the edge of the Ngorongoro crater and then far into the Serengeti plains. Julian was chased by a baboon, David was bitten by bedbugs and Hannah and Jonathan had food poisoning. Even so, I think it was our greatest and most memorable family holiday.

10

FOOD FOR THOUGHT

When I look back over our adventurous lives there's no doubt that the memories which spring most easily to mind are those involving food. When one of us struggles to recall a distant acquaintance, we only have to say 'You remember the miserable Swiss I sat next to in Mombasa and the incident of the Barracuda fish?' Or, 'You surely can't have forgotten the Chinese meal where the M.D's wife had to be carried out feet first because she'd mixed her drinks?' And of course immediately all the memories come flooding back titillating our taste-buds. 'Mm, it's been ages since we've eaten that, let's do it again tomorrow!'

The drunken Chinese meal I referred to was held in Onitsha Nigeria and was to celebrate the opening of the factory's new canteen. The company was run in partnership by the English -David was the marketing director - and the Chinese. There was a huge Chinese workforce and they only ate Chinese food. All the ingredients were shipped in from Hong Kong and frequently there would be problems with customs as prohibited dried cats were found hidden amongst the imported machinery parts. Dried cats were obviously a delicacy.

We were all invited to the grand opening and arrived that evening full of expectations. The huge room with concrete floor was filled with dozens of round tables around each of which sat ten people. When asked what I'd like to drink I said a brandy and soda. The next minute a full bottle of brandy was placed at my side. Each guest ended up with a bottle of their own particular tipple next to their glass.

Then the food started to arrive. It was superb and there were dozens of separate dishes each of which was incredibly tasty. We were all busy chattering away, eating and drinking until I realized that I'd begun to feel slightly tipsy. Since I hadn't drunk too much I wondered why. Then I saw the reason. The waiters just filled our glasses with whatever bottle they happened to have in their hands. So my drink was probably a mixture of gin, whisky and brandy. No wonder I felt strange. Halfway through the meal there was chaos and we saw the MD's Japanese wife being carried out unconscious. We decided we'd better go home. Everyone had the same thought and suddenly the room emptied. There must have been so much uneaten food left behind. But maybe that was the intention.

* * *

Nor will I ever forget the farewell dinner which was given for us in Onitsha. In fact we were only supposed to be going home on leave for six weeks but nevertheless a local chief thought he would like to honour us with a dinner party at the Phoenix Hotel. It turned out to be a somewhat bizarre experience.

The moment I saw the green neon strip lighting I should have guessed that this was to be an evening with a difference. The party was held outside on the terrace of the hotel. On one hand this was quite good as we could catch any breeze that happened to pass by, but on the other it meant that we would be bitten to death by mosquitoes. Maybe the green lights were supposed to deter the mosquitoes? In which case they failed. However they did have the most peculiar effect on the appearance of the guests. David and I, who were the only white couple there, turned a sickly Martian green whilst our African colleagues deepened into a murky shade of purple. We were offered drinks - beer or water. I chose the beer since it was probably a safer bet when it came to bacteria. It arrived in a bottle but without glasses, so drinking straight from the bottle it had to be. I was desperately thirsty as the humidity was so high that the perspiration was by then trickling down my legs into my sandals, my evening dress (life was rather formal in those days) was clinging damply to my body and my carefully straightened hair was becoming curlier and curlier by the minute.

At last it was time to sit down. The Chief leant over to me. 'My dear Mrs Matthews' he said (I hadn't the energy to correct him), 'I thought we would prepare an English dinner for you tonight.' I was deeply touched that he should have taken the trouble to try to find something that he thought would be a treat for us. But the Ibos are incredibly kind and generous people so it should have come as no surprise. 'We have decided to make you steak and kidney pie' he announced proudly. I saw David's eyes light up - one of his favourite meals!

Whilst we waited, making small talk and squashing mosquitoes, I noticed with relief that we had drinking glasses on the table. Then the plates arrived. They were pyrex and quite cold. For some strange reason they must have been kept in the fridge. This was not a good start. Several waiters appeared in their smart white and gold jackets, frayed at the sleeve and missing a button or two, and with much ceremony lowered two large pies and bowls of potatoes onto the table. It looked good. A large slice was placed on my plate. I took the first mouthful and chewed, and chewed and chewed. The meat was almost raw and not very hot - I realized that it had been cooked for the same length of time as the pastry, about half an hour would have been my guess.

There was no way I could possibly swallow the meat as it was now a large glutinous lump in my mouth. I coughed politely into my napkin, secreting the meat into one of its folds. I continued to pick at the pastry, keeping the conversation bubbling along as best I could, hoping no-one would notice the meat sliding from my plate into my napkin. By now the grease in the gravy had started to congeal on the cold plates, forming a white fatty rim. I decided that perhaps a brandy and soda might kill off any worms and bacteria I'd just ingested. If it didn't it would at least help me feel better about the situation.

In the end I resorted to lies, claiming that unfortunately the Doctor had put me on rather a strict diet. The Chief beamed consolingly, 'We have fruit salad for dessert,' he said encouragingly.

'Wonderful,' I thought. Freshly picked bananas, paw-paw, mangoes, and oranges. That would be perfect. A huge glass bowl arrived but my heart sank as I recognized the contents of several tins of canned fruit salad. It didn't make any kind of sense to me. Until of course I realized just how expensive these imported tins were. The fact that they were so expensive was the key – the Chief wanted to impress us, so therefore we couldn't be given the 'cheap' fresh fruit, but deserved the best that money could buy. I've always hated tinned fruit cocktails with their anaemic cubes of pear and pineapple and pale pink cherries like virgins' nipples. Still it was edible and probably safe. I downed another brandy and looked forward to getting home. I'd been bitten all over and was itching everywhere.

The Chief then placed his hand on my arm. 'Now,' he enquired 'are you ready for your hors d'oeuvres?' This was definitely not a question I'd been expecting.

'Oh, yes, of course' I muttered. 'Lovely.' What else could I say?

It was worse than even I could have imagined. A large plate was put in front of me and sitting in the middle was a huge raw (but thankfully peeled) onion. Next to it was a hard boiled egg and dominating the plate, a mound of cold baked beans. I tried desperately to think of topics for discussion whilst I moved the food around the plate, hoping that no-one would notice that I wasn't really eating.

At last it was time to go home and whilst it was easy to laugh in retrospect at the evening's events I had to remind myself how much thought had gone into planning what they thought was a sophisticated English dinner. But what on earth had the other guests thought of it I wondered? I suspect we'd all have been so much happier with a local palm oil or ground nut stew.

Back home we found that Ken had called round to see us. He made us laugh when he said that Raphael had been very hospitable, offering him a drink. Ken had asked for a gin and tonic and Raphael had brought him a glass of tonic water mixed with ginger ale. The missionary influence I think.

Now years later I look back with affection on that night and at so many other memorable meals in strange and wonderful places. But their magic often lay not so much in the food but in their surroundings.

* * *

It was New Year's Eve in Nigeria. The children were asleep and we sat under the ceiling fan, trying to cool off. The French windows on both sides of the room were wide open, letting in a little night breeze as well as the mosquitoes. The night was dark, hot and humid and occasionally we moved out to sit on the cool stone steps, looking up at the stars and wondering what our families and friends were doing far away in northern Europe. Then feeling restless we left the children with Rose and wandered down to the Club to see if there was anyone to have a drink with.

A few retired or out –of– work judges sat on the bar stools reliving old cases. I'd never met so many lawyers in one place. My favourite, whom I dubbed 'Judge Jeffries' raised a hand in greeting, wishing us well for the New Year. We got on well with him despite his belief that capital punishment was the solution to all crime. He at least enjoyed a good argument and took no offence at my 'liberal' ideas.

Just as we were about to leave Jonny R, an English friend who worked for a French company wandered in – like us at a loose end on what should have been a party night. In his thirties, Jonny was a tall good-looking bachelor in need of a wife. The three of us decided to go back to our house as the others were clearly glued to their seats for the next few hours and there was little sign of anything happening.

Finding 'party food' was a bit of a problem, I raided the cupboard and found a packet of pappadums and a couple of tins of 'fake' caviar which I must have bought in Lagos. The kitchen was unbelievable hot even before I started deep frying, as we had no luxuries like air-conditioning in it. Meanwhile David had opened the champagne Jonny had brought which we mixed with brandy – a heady but lethal concoction. After a few glasses we thought we might try to play a game we'd bought for Christmas called The Business Game. But either it was too complicated or we were too merry – whatever the reason (and I suspect the latter) – we failed miserably.

In the end we sat outside beneath the stars and wondered what the future held for us all. Where would we all be this time next year? At the time it seemed a rather sad celebration so far away from home but now we look back on it with great nostalgia as one of those strangely memorable and unrepeatable evenings. Every New Year's Eve since then we always think of that simple celebration with a certain longing. Now as we tuck into our eight course French New Year's Eve party in the village hall, complete with streamers and accordions, we recall with affection that splendid solitary evening. Jonny, I wonder where are you now?

* * *

The Baracuda incident took place many years later, in Mombasa, Kenya. David was visiting the office for a couple of days and one night we had some important customers to entertain. One of our guests was a very serious Swiss gentleman who rarely smiled and was very hard work. David told me that my job that evening was to get him to relax and smile.

The fish restaurant was on the edge of the white sands, beyond which the Indian Ocean moaned rhythmically but which, except for the moon's dancing reflection, was almost invisible. I sat down next to our Swiss guest and we studied the menu. 'Have you ever eaten barracuda?' he asked.

'No, I don't think so.'

'Well, you must try it, it's wonderful,' he replied. The waiter arrived, pencil poised ready to take our orders.

'I'd like some barracuda please.'

The waiter shook his head. 'We have no barracuda' he said.

I was disappointed but saw that ' fish of the day' was on offer. 'What's the fish of the day?'

'Barracuda' he replied.

I was confused. Still this was Africa so I said 'Ok, I'll have the barracuda.'

'We have no barracuda' he said again.

'But you just said it was the fish of the day!'

'If you want barracuda, you ask for fish of the day' he replied.

I took a deep breath. 'Fish of the day please.'

"Ok," he said. 'One barracuda.'

I looked at my Swiss neighbour. He not only smiled he laughed!

11

DAR -ES –SALAAM
THE HAVEN OF PEACE

Twenty five years after leaving Ghana, we touched down yet again in Nairobi where most of the passengers disembarked. David had continued to work in Africa during the intervening years, but had been based for the most part in London. However I had been lucky enough to have been able to travel frequently with him around the world, but mostly to the African continent where his job, this time not in textiles but in earth moving equipment, had brought us back time and again, to the wide plains and cities of East, South and West Africa.

As we came into land I gazed down over the empty plains below, dotted here and there with lone acacias and crossed with animal and vehicle tracks. Despite so many visits my heart still lurched, as I gazed at the five knuckles of the Ngong hills which punched the skyline with their clenched fist.

Nearer to, the modern skyline of the city shone in the early morning sun and it was hard to believe that only a little more than a hundred years ago, this thriving modern city had been a one-hotel watering stop for the great Mombasa to Uganda railway line.

Today however, we were not stopping in Kenya. We were heading off firstly to Tanzania, then across into Uganda and finally back into Kenya to say our final farewells. After forty years David was making his last visit to a continent which had been the centre of his working life. I thought at the time that it was to be mine too.

After an hour and half we took off again, turning south-east towards Dar-es-Salaam. The Captain flew us right over the top of Mount Kilimanjaro, Africa's tallest mountain and I was amazed to see how little snow was left and how clearly the crater stood out – a deflated chocolate bun, streaked with frosted icing. Maybe one day soon, as a result of global warming, there will be no snow at all.

An hour later we landed in Dar, which lay sweltering on the edge of the Indian Ocean. As we flew out to sea before turning back to line up with the runway, I remembered my first hair-raising flight to Dar, in an old crate belonging to Air Tanzania. The stewardess had been so fat she could hardly squeeze down the aisle. But she was friendly and looked rather hurt when I declined the food, settling instead for a bottle of water. The last thing I had needed on the journey ahead were constant emergency stops. Especially since the only loos available would be bushes.

I suppose this was my fourth visit to Dar and I had been told that at last the city was getting itself together and was now a little less chaotic. It didn't take long to get through immigration (this time David didn't have to fiddle the date on my health certificate) and Taju's smiling face was waiting to greet us. Taju was a tall, gentle bespectacled Nigerian Muslim who now ran the Tanzania branch of the company. He'd left his family behind in Nigeria, seeing them only rarely. Yet it was the choice he had made. The Europeans who had previously held the job had taken their families with them and built themselves a new life together.

But separateness is not uncommon in many African cultures. Often parents leave their children in the family village with aunts or grandparents while they find better paid work in the cities, maybe only seeing their children once or twice a year.

We piled into the car and our old friend and driver, Shibani who'd been with the company for many years, drove us to the Sheraton which had been built since my last visit. But first Taju told us that we had to call at the office. David and I looked at one another. Did this mean that some sort of reception had been organized? I hoped not, as I would find an organized goodbye too painful.

Fortunately everyone had gone for lunch and Taju alone presented us with a beautiful and ornately carved Zanzibar chest, a farewell gift from the company in Tanzania. It now rests at the foot of our bed, a daily reminder of that other haven of peace.

I was surprised to see the modern high-rise Sheraton looming over the faded colonial buildings, the phallic minarets. It seemed strangely incongruous. Our room was on the 6th floor, its huge double glazed windows shutting out the sounds and smells, but giving us a panoramic view of the turquoise pool far below. Tiny white bodies stretched out on blue and white sun-beds, like numerals around a clock-face. While I unpacked something to wear for the official company dinner, David showered and left for the office – his last meeting with the staff. For a time I lay on the bed, listening to the drone of the air-conditioner, its chill cooling my skin. I tried to sleep because that evening I would have to be lively for I guessed the conversation at dinner would be somewhat stilted. I wasn't sure whether any other wives had been invited and I knew for certain that the men would feel happier talking among themselves.

I couldn't settle though, the thrill of being in Africa once again and the thought of the arduous journey ahead, kept the adrenalin racing through my veins. So instead, I decided to shower and explore the hotel.

I made my way down to the poolside and pulled a sun-bed partially under the shade of a large striped umbrella. Maybe a swim and the fresh air would make me drowsy. But I was surrounded by loud British voices and laughter. I realized then that most of them were the crew from our flight. After a while the endless banter began to irritate me – this was not what I had come for - so I wandered off, finally returning to our room.

On previous visits we had stayed with Paul and Liz and then Rolf and Sarah in their homes. I had really loved seeing how they lived, doing the shopping, taking the children to school, walking around the garden and soaking up a different sort of life. Sharing someone's home even for a short time opens up new horizons, reveals different lifestyles. A kind of acceptable voyeurism – a taste of what might have been had we chosen to work permanently overseas.

David eventually returned and at 7.00 p.m. we went downstairs to meet Taju who must have been starving. As a devout Muslim he was observing Ramadan, which meant that during the day he could neither eat nor drink, and in the heat and humidity of Dar that must have been a real test of will-power. But between now and sunrise he could eat all he wanted.

Dinner was to be at **The Alcove** in the centre of town. Bouncing up and down along the pot-holed roads I had a chance to get a closer look at the chaos called Dar. A newcomer would still be aghast at the dust and decay, the crumbling colonial buildings, the litter strewn broken pavements. But there was a new energy about the city. People seemed to move faster and the food stalls had more than a small pyramid of misshapen tomatoes to offer. Small roadside fires grilled meat kebabs and hurricane lamps flickered against mud-spattered walls.

As we drew up to the restaurant, a combined Chinese and Indian, I thought how different Dar must have looked in its hey-day when the Aly Khan had built Rita Hayworth a home on the fabulous palm-lined Oyster Bay.

Upstairs the team were already there, with bottles of beer placed like sentries down the centre of the table. Taju, had not invited any wives. I suppose since many of the men would have had more than one, this could have caused some domestic headaches. Although at some parties in the past we had invited the number one wife, which had worked out quite well. However he'd brought along Esther his secretary to keep me company. She was very liberated and great fun, and I think both the men and I were relieved not to have to make polite conversation.

Of all the African countries we had visited, I'd found the Tanzanian women the most shy and self-effacing. I remember a drinks party held for us one evening at Rolf's house when all the Tanzanian wives had retreated to a corner of the terrace and lined up in a row. I'd walked along the line, shaking hands and trying to get some sort of conversation going. 'How many children do you have?' 'Which village do you come from?' It wasn't a success and I think both they and I were relieved when I finally slipped away and left them to talk to one another. The British High Commissioner had been invited too and far from being stuffy, was relaxed and great fun with a store of less than diplomatic revelations.

As I sat down at the head of the table, I realized how ravenously hungry I was. We hadn't eaten since the tasteless chicken brioche on the previous night's flight. Now some twenty hours later, I tucked into chicken legs, prawns, spring rolls and then a superb fish curry. Living on the edge of the Indian Ocean definitely has its advantages.

The only other white face at the table was that of P.A., whose interesting and colourful life of sexual conquests never ceased to amaze me. I remembered meeting him and his wife not long after they were married. They were full of excitement and working hard to cope with a strange new life overseas. But too much free time and too much money can put a lot of pressure on relationships and soon there had been gossip concerning both of them. Then I heard that she had been caught in a compromising position with a Frenchman in the ladies' room at the club, which caused much scandal and gossip. She had returned home to

England and they eventually divorced. A couple of years later he'd gone through some kind of marriage ceremony with a local lady in another African country. Apparently he'd then left her when he was posted elsewhere. I was told her family were still trying to get justice. What a mess. I wonder where he is now and how many other lives have been ruined in his wake? It would make a great story.

I think everyone was relieved to get to the end of the evening and at ten we all left and piled into the row of company 4x4s and pick-ups which lined the road outside. The next morning Moses, the company Personnel Manager would escort us to Zanzibar for the day. Being a non-Muslim, he had no need to observe Ramadan and so could join us for lunch. So we said a temporary goodbye to Taju, whom we would see the day after that, when he was to come with us to Lake Victoria, then onwards through western Kenya and as far as the Ugandan border.

1973 Onitsha, Hannah, Julian and Jonathan

1996 The house in Onitsha, with its mature gardens

1974 Accra, David's parents, Edith and John on holiday with us

1996 Our house in Accra, empty and awaiting demolition

1973 Onitsha – David and the boys at the wedding of
Stan and Esther

1973 Obi and me with children and friends

*1996 David in Zanzibar with baskets of dates and
below 1974 David and me at Adda*

12

The Spice Islands

What exotic images spring to mind whenever Zanzibar is mentioned – white sands, turquoise seas, fragrant spices and ornate Arab architecture. It is all of these things of course, but it is overlaid with dirt, decay, and lethargy. And at its centre stand incongruous concrete apartment blocks, courtesy of East Germany. The first time I saw them I was horrified that anything so ugly could have been built on such an idyllic island.

This was my second visit, my first had been a few years earlier when we had stayed with Rolf and Sarah, and had flown in a minute plane, forgetting to take our health certificates. Although Zanzibar is part of Tanzania it likes to think of itself as independent – or at least semi autonomous – so we needed both passports and health certificates as there was still the fear of Yellow Fever. At first we were refused entry, but then our Tanzanian colleague had a few private words, no doubt a large 'dash' was handed out and we were free to enter. In Africa most problems are surmountable....

This time however, we were to go by local ferry which would be much more fun. Moses was waiting in the hotel foyer for us at 7.00 a.m. His appearance suggested that his favourite pastime was eating and drinking. He was as broad as he was tall. His skin was blue black, and his smile was wide and friendly and he moved slowly, restricted by his stature. A few years ago he'd spent time in police custody being investigated for misappropriation of hospital goods. As a member of the local hospital governing board he was alleged to have sold off the linen. He was never charged, but as I said, most problems in Africa...

The town was already bustling with activity – the roads heaving with overloaded lorries – and the once orderly German pavements, thronging with bodies, noise and confusion. Down by the ferry terminal the ticket offices were besieged by hopeful travellers. A few were back-packers, but most were locals staggering under huge bundles perched precariously on their heads. I spotted a few business men clutching smart briefcases, no doubt civil servants, of whom there are millions. I don't think there is another country that outclasses Tanzania when it comes to bureaucracy. Although France runs it a close second.

Because we were too early to be allowed through to the waiting area, David and I did a quick walk around the town., dodging taxis, potholes and broken paving stones. Even at this early hour the traders were at their stalls, shops were open and Dar was bristling with activity. The old German colonial buildings had lost their grandeur. Their faded facades were tarnished with dirt and neglect. Paint peeled from the plastered walls, shutters hung off rusty hinges, windows were cracked and unwashed. But inside the buildings you could sense a new vitality, and I could feel that the city had a more determined air than it had on my last visit.

Returning to the terminal we wandered down the wooden walkway and were herded into an open air waiting area, where we sat on wooden benches beneath a tin roof. Next to me sat two young blonde German brothers, with identical profiles. Opposite a middle-aged Tanzanian clutched his briefcase tightly to his chest. Suddenly he stood up, his case fell to the floor and out spilt his dirty washing and an old newspaper.

Once allowed on board we were shown to the first class lounge with its freezing air-conditioning and windows streaming with condensation. The seats outside looked much more fun. The senior crew were all white, the roly-poly Captain in white and gold was Norwegian and the two engineers English. No doubt down below there were some local Tanzanians, and soon one appeared to offer us coffee. It arrived in plastic cups and we were each given a whole packet of biscuits. An excellent breakfast. I wandered up onto the deck and watched the last passengers come aboard. Stepping around the bundles and bicycles I photographed the port and chatted to the engineer who came from Newcastle. He'd previously worked for Stena Lines and had only been in Africa for two weeks. He was still finding his feet, he said, and was struggling to discover how the system worked. I told him that the system was that there was no system. And that is the frustration and joy of Africa.

We were due to sail at 8.00 a.m. But this was of course Africa and we discovered that the fuel which should have been delivered last night had not yet arrived. But it was 'on its way'! Translated that meant 'We haven't the faintest idea where it is, but I know this answer should keep you happy'. By 9.00 we were beginning to get anxious. Our return journey was booked for 3.00 p.m. which would allow us a couple of hours for lunch and a walk around the market, providing of course that we left the mainland before 10.00 a.m. Otherwise we would have to abort, and as this would no doubt my last visit to Zanzibar I was anxious not to miss it.

At 9.30 a.m. the tanker arrived, having been stuck in traffic outside the port. David and I walked back onto the quayside and watched the fuel being pumped into the tanks. Then at precisely 10.00 a.m. the boat's engines growled into life and we pulled away from the quay to begin our journey to Zanzibar Island which lay twenty-five miles away.

I went up on top to photograph the disappearing skyline of Dar and the waterside fish market, where in the year of the first Gulf War we had shopped with Paul and Liz for supper. It was a time when all Americans working in Africa had been sent home for fear of reprisals. But for us it meant that wherever we went we were free from other visitors. The greatest thrill was to have had the whole of the Ngorongoro Crater to ourselves. The Chief Ranger who turned out to be a cousin of David's Sales Manager in Tanzania, came with us and took us to places forbidden to tourists - we were even charged by a rhino which at the time was somewhat scary, but later a great conversation piece.

The market was as busy as I remembered it, the fishing boats pulled up on the beach, the shaky straw-roofed stalls groaning under the weight of the finest Indian Ocean fish. All that was missing from this distance was the intoxicating sea smell of fresh fish. We swept past *dhows* heading towards the shore, bobbing wildly in the turquoise wake of the ferry. But as we left the mainland behind the winds became increasingly uncomfortable, so I went back down below to people watch and read the local paper.

In front of us sat an American couple with a small girl aged about two. He spoke in a loud voice about stocks and shares, referring all the time to a two day old Wall Street Journal. She silently nodded, more interested in breastfeeding her daughter. A few minutes after setting sail, the little girl threw up, all over her mother and the floor. The Captain came below with two attractive young Tanzanian girls whom he plied with coffee and coca-cola.

An hour and three-quarters later we approached the port of Zanzibar Island. The sea was a clear bright emerald whipped to turquoise by the boat's propellers. The island's skyline was a collage of palm trees, minarets, faded elegant buildings and shanty town shacks. For centuries the island had lured traders, adventurers, plunderers and explorers to its shores. The earliest visitors were the Arab traders who sailed with the Monsoon winds and discovered the islands in the eighth century. Then came the Assyrians, Sumerians, Egyptians, Phoenicians, Indians, Chinese, Persians and Europeans. But it was the Shirazi Persians and Omani Arabs who finally settled and ruled. Under their influence the Islands became, and remain, predominantly Islamic.

The quay was jammed with passengers waiting to make the return journey, while everyone on board tried to get off at the same time across one narrow shaky gangplank. Pushed and shoved from every direction it was difficult to avoid being tipped down the stairs from the top deck. But with David grabbing my hand and pulling firmly, I finally stepped onto the quayside where Moses was already waiting for us.

Swept along with the crowd we made our way to the immigration hut, darting in and out of the port traffic, dodging huge containers, neatly side-stepping the bikes and taxi touts. Then having finished the formalities we grabbed a battered taxi to take us to the Marine Club hotel where Moses had booked for lunch.

Because it was Ramadan eating between the hours of sunrise and sunset was forbidden for all Muslims, and even non-Muslims could not be seen publicly flouting the laws. Moses, our Mr Fix-It, told us that he had found this hotel which would happily feed us. I feared it would be one of the many new modern tourist hotels which were now springing up all over the island.

Imagine my delight when we drove out of town, past the ruins of the Sultan's Harem's baths and along the spice road. Cloves had first been introduced in 1818 and flourished in the tropical climate. By the middle of the 19th century the Zanzibar archipelago was the world's largest producer of cloves, as well as producing cinnamon, cumin, ginger, pepper and cardamom. Their rich fragrance became synonymous with the Zanzibar archipelago, which became known as The Spice Islands.

The taxi drew up outside a long thatched building beneath palm trees, on the edge of the beach. It was straight out of a Bounty Bar ad. We sat outside on the narrow wooden verandah at a small table, in the middle of which a brilliant spray of scarlet hibiscus exploded from an old glass jar. Above, the palm fronds rustled in the sea breeze and beyond the cool shadows of the palms the sand was blinding white, its edges licked rhythmically by the clear aquamarine sea. We were in the middle of a long curving bay. To the north lay the town and the port and we watched a distant cruise liner nudge gently into its berth. To the south, native dug-outs lay motionless on the beach, whilst out at sea three fishermen rode the waves in home-made canoes, bobbing up and down, trawling their fishing nets in behind them.

It would be hard to have imagined a more perfect setting for lunch. I sank back into my chair and waited for the first course – a large platter of seafood salad. Even today I can taste the fresh sea taste, the tang of salt and seaweed. After that came the biggest dish of lobsters I had ever seen. Freshly grilled with butter, they were absolutely delicious. I managed two of them and David and Moses finished off the rest.

A few more visitors had turned up, a couple of back-packers in shorts and t-shirts and then some middle- aged couples dressed in what the Americans call smart-casual. By my standard they were very smart indeed. It took me a few minutes to realize that they were passengers from a cruise liner and were sporting their expensive leisure wear.

After lunch David and I decided to stroll along the beach and down towards the fishing canoes. Moses said he'd stay where he was. Exercise and Moses did not go together. Carrying my sandals in my hand I gingerly stepped across the burning sands until I reached the firmer, cooler sea fringe. The sun was almost directly overhead, but its fierce rays were tempered by the sea breeze and we walked for half an hour in what must have been near paradise. We scoured the high-tide mark for shells, but most were holed, and no doubt the young boys had scavenged before us and the best would now be for sale in the market. But shells, like fossils can never be bought, only collected. Each time I look at my shell and butterfly collection at home, I'm transported back to the 70's and the weekend jaunts in West Africa when we set off into the forests in search of butterflies or trudged along the seashore collecting sand dollars, our cold box full of chicken legs, hard-boiled eggs, mangoes, paw-paw and bananas. Those are memories which cannot be bought.

Suddenly, trapped between old rope, seaweed and a plastic bottle, lay a beautiful spiny shell – intact and absolutely perfect. It now sits on my study shelf, and I have only to pick it up to feel once more that idyllic sea breeze and vibrant sun. I felt then that the afternoon was complete, and somewhat reluctantly we wandered back, splashing through the warm sea, soaking up the sights and smells of this tropical island which we would never see again.

Moses was still sitting at the table where we'd left him. I went to the ladies room to wash the sand off my feet and then the taxi arrived and we set off towards the port, first calling at the market. There is something compelling and addictive about African markets where the smell, the colours, the hustle and bustle and ritual bargaining are so seductive.

It was very hot and sticky away from the sea breeze but despite the afternoon heat and humidity the market was full of people. And what a diversity of skin colour and bone structure. Years of intermarriage have produced a very beautiful people, their skin tones ranging from golden to dusky black. In their high cheek bones, slender noses and slim build could be seen their Arab forebears. Their black eyes, curly hair and full mouths spoke of their African ancestors. There were few women around and those who were scurried by, heads bent beneath their black headscarves, revealing only a tantalizing Arabic profile.

Goods were piled high on ramshackle stalls or laid out in neat pyramids on cloth or woven mats on the ground. Mountains of scarlet tomatoes vied with yellow peppers, ripe bananas, green oranges and juicy limes. The smell of spices saturated the air. Because it was Ramadan every stall groaned with plump shiny dates. You could even buy your dates in baskets woven from green banana leaves. If I lived there I should no doubt spend all my time shopping, cooking and eating. Though if I'm honest I seem to anyway.

As I stepped over litter strewn pavements, asking permission to photograph their goods, I suddenly felt self-conscious wandering around with bare legs and arms. I wondered how they must see us. Was our money welcomed as a means to a better lifestyle or were we condemned as offensive to their culture? I suspect a combination of the two. We drove slowly back to the port along the pot-holed roads weaving in and out between battered cars and lorries. Half-starved mangy donkeys pulled over-loaded carts and bicycles wobbled precariously as their owners tried to steer their loads away from the stinking storm drains.

Sadly we had no time to visit the historic Stone Town, the old city of Zanzibar with its strangely unromantic name. Little has changed in two hundred years and I remembered vividly from my first visit its winding alleys, its narrow bustling streets and above all its beautiful studded, carved wooden doors, a testament to the artistry and skill of its craftsmen. Most of the houses had been built in the 19th century by Arabs, British administrators and prosperous Indian businessmen, at a time when Zanzibar was one of the most important trading post in the Indian Ocean region. One of the most famous was perhaps the house given to Dr Livingstone from where he planned his final expedition into the interior. Two years later his body had been carried back to the Island by faithful servants, before his body sailed to England and its final resting place in Westminster Abbey. Many of the old buildings are now in a poor state of repair for they were built from the local coralline rock which is so easily eroded. However plans were in progress to restore the town to its original splendour. I just hope they don't wait too long.

Back at the port we made our way to the quay and joined a huge crowd patiently waiting under the shade of a tin roof. I couldn't understand why suddenly I felt so unsteady, and hoped that the lunch time seafood salad had been fresh. But then I realized that we were standing on a floating pontoon and that we were all swaying gently in time with the waves.

I squeezed onto a wooden bench next to a beautiful local girl, dressed in vivid blue and gold, and clutching several large packages. She smiled and moved over to make more room for me. Looking around the crowd I could see it was once again, a mixture of locals, back-packers and a few white businessmen.

As I gazed out to sea I thought about the island's tortured past. What a turbulent history it had had and what tragedies had taken place under its burning skies. How many thousands of slaves had been captured from the hinterlands of East Africa and herded into the dungeons of Zanzibar to wait for the ships to take them to foreign lands? These proud people had been betrayed by Europeans, Arabs and most tragically of all, their own race.

Caravans starting out from Bagamoyo on the mainland coast, had traveled as much as 1,000 miles on foot - as far as Lake Tankanyika - buying slaves from local rulers or simply capturing them en route. Chained by their necks they were led back to the coast, carrying with them tons of ivory from slaughtered elephants.

The name Bagamoyo means 'lay down your heart' for it was here that the slaves would abandon all hope of freedom. It was not until 1873, when the local Sultan was threatened with a British naval bombardment, that the Slave Market was closed down and the sea-borne slave trade finally came to an end. The Cathedral Church of Christ now stands on the site of the old slave market.

When the hovercraft finally arrived there was a great surge forward as we all tried to squeeze onto the gangplank. Moses had disappeared from sight and David who had the tickets was ahead of me. He stretched out a hand above the heads of the pushing crowd and tried to pull me along with him. An old lady behind had a huge bundle on her head which, since she was several inches shorter than me, kept swinging into my back. Someone else's suitcase battered into the backs of my knees, causing my legs to buckle.

Eventually we made it. Moses was already seated, no doubt having used his bulk as a battering ram. We found two seats at the front of the boat but it was so hot I could scarcely breathe. The air-conditioning was not working of course and I wondered with alarm how we were all going to survive for the next one and a half hours. But I needn't have worried for as we set off a good strong breeze came in from the open doors. I turned to watch the disappearing skyline and hoped that the picture before me would always stay bright and clear in my mind.

Moses had struck up a conversation with some local Asians who were in the construction business and they were all busy exchanging cards. I closed my eyes and tried to forget the cramped conditions and bumpy seas. I congratulated myself on pinching a sick bag from the morning's ferry. At least I could cope with one end if necessary. I was now longing to get back to the hotel for a cool shower, a change of clothes and a good night's sleep. Not forgetting a large gin and tonic. The excitement and anticipation of the outward journey had been replaced by tiredness and irritability.

A few miles out of Dar the boat suddenly slowed down, almost to a halt. I groaned at the thought of engine failure and a night spent on the high seas. Nothing was said as we were tossed about in the turbulent waters. About ten minutes later a huge launch swept past with much hooting, leaving us bobbing like a plastic duck. Later we were told that it had been the President returning from Zanzibar with a foreign dignitary. We followed slowly behind and arrived half an hour late. Shabani was waiting patiently for us, and so we said our goodbyes and thanks to Moses who was already planning his career in politics. His experience with the missing hospital linen suggested he was undoubtedly well qualified.

What a difference a hot shower and gin and tonic can make. Tomorrow we were to fly to Lake Victoria, then drive up the east coast of the lake cross the border into Kenya where we would stay overnight in Kisumu at the northern end of the lake The following day we would head into Uganda and then drive north to the Victoria Nile, for me a new and unknown region.

I knew that we were in for some excitement and some discomfort as the journey would take us through some tough and inhospitable regions. But that was what I had come for.

13

MWANZA - LAKE VICTORIA

Hardly had my head touched the pillow when a piercing alarm told us it was 4.30 a.m. Was Zanzibar really only yesterday? We staggered reluctantly from bed, washed and collected our now dried underwear and socks and packed up our grips. Because they were to be checked in we had to padlock everything, otherwise we'd probably lose most of our clothes. Even so I carried my contact lens and a spare pair of pants in my handbag, so that I could manage the next day if the luggage went missing. Once when we had flown from Johannesburg to Nairobi our luggage had gone to Harare, and we'd spent two nights stripping off our clothes, washing them and putting them back on the next day, still slightly damp. It was not to be recommended.

At 5.00 a.m. we met Taju in the lobby and set off, with Shabani driving, to the airport. Looking out of the window I tried hard to imprint it all to memory for this would be my last visit to Dar-es-Salaam. I can't bear to think of any experience as being the last, it's an admission of mortality. But I suppose one of the few advantages of age is that it gets easier to accept the inevitable.

At the airport we said goodbye to Shibani thanking him for all the help and kindness he had shown over the years. As the sky lightened we checked-in. Although our tickets entitled us to sit in the first class lounge, it was claustrophobic with its TV tuned loudly to CNN and its plastic sofas covered in frilly pink satin cushions. I went to collect some free coffee and then wandered around to watch our fellow passengers. Taju was not able to drink or eat anything now until after sunset, and we were concerned for him, as the journey ahead was to be long, hot and dusty.

After an hour's delay we eventually boarded and took off into a brilliant sky for the hour- long flight to Mwanza, which lies at the southern end of Lake Victoria.

David slept whilst I gazed below at the changing contours of the African landscape, the deep earthy tones of her undulating hills and dried out river beds. I tried to imagine how those first explorers must have felt seeing the vastness of the landscape, feeling the intensity of its heat. It was at Mwanza that Speke first saw Lake Victoria in 1858 and recognized it as the source of the Nile. Now it's become a busy town supporting an ever growing population.

At the airport we were met by William Molulu our local sales manager who was waiting in the company 4x4 to drive us north to the Kenyan border, some five hours away. William was smartly dressed, charming, friendly and eager to please. He decided that we must be related since our name, pronounced in the African way, sounded very like his. It was an interesting theory.

We had arranged to be at the Kenyan border for 3.00 p.m. where we would be met by Julius who was the western Kenya sales manager based in Kisumu. There we were to spend the night before heading off to the Ugandan border, where we would be met by Andy the Nigerian head of the Ugandan business. Such a cosmopolitan company! Then with him and his wife Clara, whom we would collect in Kampala, the capital of Uganda, we would head north towards the Murchison Falls and the Victoria Nile.

There was some hard driving ahead of us over the next few days. The roads that had once been tarmac would certainly be pot-holed and eroded making the journey slow and uncomfortable. But others would simply be dirt tracks, their deep ruts baked dry or axle deep in mud. It would all depend on how much rain there had been.

Whilst we waited in a shoddy bare room for our luggage to be unloaded I chatted to a young Dutch boy who was visiting Africa for the first time to see his fiancée, a nurse at the local hospital. How exciting the experience must have been for him.

If only we could have traded ages and experiences, what luxury for us both. And then at 9.15.a.m. bags stacked behind the back seat, we set off for the border post at Sarari.

Heading out of town we caught our first sight of Lake Victoria, which is more like a sea than a lake. Also known as Victoria Nyanza, it is the largest lake in Africa, the world's largest tropical lake and the second largest lake in the world - in surface area. It covers 68,800 sq km and has a coastline of 3,330 sq km.

The area is one of the most densely populated regions in Africa, and the millions of people who live within 50 miles of the Lake, rely heavily on the 200 species of fish which are caught by local fishermen. Not only do the fish provide a large part of their diet, but their export makes a major contribution to the economy. In the 1960's Nile Perch was introduced into the lake but since then has unfortunately overwhelmed the other species of fish. Huge canning factories had been built on the lake shores, and whilst they provided work directly and indirectly for thousands, they had also brought great problems to the area. Workers were housed in basic unhygienic conditions and the remains of the fish, after the filleting process were often dumped some miles away in the open air. The lake itself had become increasingly polluted.

We were shocked to see how the dreaded water hyacinth had taken hold, massing in each inlet and bay, making it impossible for the fishermen to launch their canoes. Since the weed doubles in size every twenty-seven days drastic steps would need to be taken to control its spread. We had learnt during our visit the previous year to Lake Kariba in Zimbabwe that conservationists were hoping to introduce a beetle which would eat the roots and curb the weed's growth.

We turned north, passing a plot of ground between the road and the lake where small white crosses, scattered beneath the trees, marked the burial places of those bodies which had been found after the previous year's ferry disaster. Sadly not all the three hundred bodies were recovered. The crocodiles here were very well fed.

The lake soon disappeared from our view, even though we continued to run parallel to it. The landscape became an undulating dusty red, with stark rock outcrops erupting from the parched earth. Huge boulders balanced precariously on one another and it seemed that the gentlest of pushes would have caused them to topple. In reality they had been there for thousands of years, and perhaps for thousands more to come.

William was anxious to please us and suggested that instead of driving straight to the border, we could turn east into the Serengeti pan handle, without losing much time. He knew a track, he said, which would take us out northwards and link us back to the border road. Both David and I had visited the Serengeti many times, but neither of us had explored the pan handle and thought it a great idea, so readily agreed.

Of course nothing in Africa is straightforward. Turning off the road we headed east and paused briefly at the small hut where we registered our entry into the wilderness. I decided this was a good time to commune with nature as I may not have another opportunity for a long time. So wandering nonchalantly away from the car, hopefully giving the impression that I was bird-watching, I slipped gratefully behind a large bush (having first checked for snakes). As I struggled to pull up my shorts I came face to face with an old man who was walking barefoot along the track. In some respects life is a lot easier for men.

Back in the car I now felt able to take a mouthful of water. William refused a banana which we had bought from a roadside seller, and I couldn't even offer one to Taju. But David and I had decided that it was lunchtime. Last night's dinner in Dar seemed a long time ago and Tanzanian bananas are deliciously small and sweet, so unlike the large raw variety that we eat at home.

The Serengeti pan handle is exactly what it says – a narrow corridor of wilderness stretching westwards from the wide plains towards the lake. In the dry season millions of animals migrate along it in search of water. It is a remote and isolated area far from the vast grasslands which normally attract visitors. Because of its isolation it can also be dangerous and the previous year an overland truck had been attacked by bandits one night, killing some tourists. We drove for a long time in this most beautiful of landscapes, only once seeing two German cars heading towards a distant campsite.

David was now becoming concerned because not only had we turned east, but we were also clearly heading south. After some time he asked William 'When do we start heading north?' William replied 'Not long, about another hour!' David and I exchanged glances. Taju said nothing. I looked at my watch, it was now 1.00 p.m. We were supposed to be at the border about 3.00 p.m. and we were still driving in the wrong direction. William himself had clearly become a little anxious and realized he'd bitten off more than he could chew.

The dusty tracks were very bumpy and we were flung wildly about, often hitting our heads on the car roof, as William pressed the accelerator to the floor. The air-conditioning had packed up so we had to open the windows which meant that we were now covered in a film of fine red dust. But at least the temperature was bearable. The dust collected in our throats and we needed to take frequent swigs of water to wash out our mouths. This was a tricky manoeuvre since the car was lurching from side to side and of course we both ended up rather wet.

But the journey was worth the discomfort. How I love the Serengeti, its enormous skies, endless horizons and the delicate hues of its golden grasses. Slender gazelles grazed or sheltered beneath the magnificent acacias, their limpid eyes and flickering ears ever watchful for predators. Stately giraffes languidly munched the tops of thorn trees, a lone male buffalo pawed the dusty earth menacingly. But there was no time to stop, to cut the engine, to listen to the silence and smell the rich tang of dust and decay. For me the greatest thrill is to have the wilderness to myself and that day, between us and the horizon there was no sign of human life.

'How far to the border now, William?' David asked. 'About two hours' was the reply. Things were not looking good. Soon we came across an armed guard and William stopped to speak to him. The news was worse than we expected. All the bridges had been swept away in the recent floods and our only solution was to turn back and find another way out.

When we eventually rejoined the border- bound road, we discovered that we were only a few miles from where we'd turned off. The small detour had taken us four hours and a sharp decline in David's patience. But I thought it had been worth every minute and every bruise.

Now it was a race against time as we headed north towards the Kenyan border. William had clearly become agitated, hunching over the steering wheel and pressing hard on the accelerator. Then he told us why. 'We must get through this area before dark', he warned us. 'This is a very hostile area, full of bandits. The Kuria are very dangerous people'. And just when I thought everything was going smoothly. Still, I felt reasonably sanguine. After all if they pinched the 4x4 someone would not doubt come and get us, wouldn't they? 'Oh no' William said. 'They kill you'.

He then went on to tell us how before the young men of this particular tribe can marry they have to kill a human, as the

Maasai used to have to kill a lion. Now this bit of information put a different complexion on things. Just how reliable was William's story? I looked at the position of the sun and then at my watch. Night in this part of the world comes quite early. But I worked out that with a bit of luck we could just make the border before dark.

Despite warning glares from David, William was now in full flight, padding out his stories with gruesome details. Maybe it helped relieve his tension. It certainly didn't relieve mine. How ironic it would be if after all the years of travelling in remote places we were to finally meet our fate on our farewell tour. The most dangerous area was still ahead of us William kindly informed us, pointing at the narrow pass which climbed around the approaching rocky hillside. This apparently was the favoured place for ambushes. As we climbed higher, my heart skipped a beat with each bend. But then as the sun began to slip away so did my fears.

A kind of weary acceptance stole over me and I suddenly felt quite calm. You can only die once, I thought, and it would probably be quick. The children were adults and self-sufficient, the mortgage was paid off and I'd had a damn good life. With that comforting thought I concentrated on admiring the arid countryside and thought wistfully of a long, cool alcoholic drink.

Just before sunset we finally arrived at Sarari the border post and pulled up at the small tin customs hut and road barrier.

The area was completely deserted. A solitary soldier appeared and seeing the company logo on our 4x4 informed us that our Kenyan driver had been waiting for us all day, but had given up and gone away. This was depressing news. I climbed out of the car, my legs still shaking from the hours of bouncing up and down. There was still heat in the sinking sun and I lay my head back against a wooden post and anticipated a night spent at the border crossing. The reason for having a Kenyan car to meet us was the difficulty and bureaucracy involved in taking a Tanzanian car into another country.

David, Taju and William had disappeared but eventually came back with the good news that provided we left the registration papers with the guard, William could take us on to Kisumu and return the following day. Most problems in Africa….

But just at that moment Julius and the Kenyan company car turned up. He'd been to the next village to find a phone and let the office know that we had not arrived. Poor Julius was hyper-agitated, wavering between relief and irritation. For some unknown reason he'd been told to expect us at 10.00 a.m., five hours before our planned arrival time. Now the P&T office (Post & Telegraph) was closed, so he couldn't let our colleague David Hipkin know that we were safe. My heart sank when he told us there was still another three hour journey ahead.

So we said farewell to William who insisted on having his photograph taken with us. We all squinted into the evening sunlight tired, dishevelled and dusty, posing against the T&E logo. No doubt the photograph will end up in an old box and in a few years his children will wonder who we were. And even William will have forgotten.

Before we could set off we had to negotiate immigration. David gave me both passports as it's usually easier for a female to charm her way through. Taju came along with his passport and with Julius as support. The tiny hut consisted of a dusty room with a tin roof and concrete floor. In the corner was an old table behind which an officious little man thumbed his way pedantically through a pile of yellowing papers. Taking my passport he scrutinized my photograph and then turned each page slowly, reading every visa entry that had been stamped in over the last few years. A fly buzzed frantically around the room. A young girl shuffled in, her worn flip-flops splattering on the concrete floor. No-one spoke.

The official suddenly flicked back a few pages of my passport, glanced at me again over the top of his metal spectacles, as though he had discovered some damning evidence. I tried to remain calm although inside I was silently screaming with frustration. I was exhausted from being thrown around the car for hours. What I needed was to get out of there and back on the road in search of my bed. Finally he stamped both our passports and handed them back without saying a word.

He saved his most officious pomposity for poor Taju. The trouble is that Nigerians have such a terrible reputation for corruption and Taju was about to unfairly bear the consequences of his country's misdemeanours. The hut was filled with a tense silence as Mr. Immigration licked his finger and slowly scrutinized every page, twisting the passport in his hand to check the entry stamps, the visas, the work permit. He was determined to show who was boss and it took half an hour of cross examination before he agreed to let Taju enter Kenya. Both Taju and Julius kept their cool and even I kept my silence. By no means a small achievement, but I'd learnt long ago that there are no prizes for arguing with officials

14

UGANDA
THE PEARL OF AFRICA

We emerged into the fading light, climbed into the car and set off for Kisumu which lies at the northern tip of Lake Victoria. We had only moved into second gear when Julius announced that, since all the large roads were dangerous at night because of the bandits, we'd have to make a detour along the lakeside route. And just when I thought we'd left all the anxieties behind.

We were by now, all extremely tired, dirty and hungry. Taju must have been starving since he'd neither eaten nor drunk anything all day. The thought of another three hours bumping along dirt-tracks and potholes filled me with despair. But I had known beforehand that this trip was going to be a hard one, so there was nothing I could do except take a deep breath and dream of a long hot bath and a soft bed.

But as usual there were always compensations and it was fascinating to drive through the small lakeside villages where food stalls, lit by candles and hurricane lamps, were busy with evening customers and where the distant hills on the far side of the lake, flickered with the tongues of sporadic fires. Why do I love it so?

When at last I saw the far-off lights of Kisumu across the water I felt a sense of elation. At last a luxurious bath, clean clothes and dinner. But then Julius told us it would take at least another hour to drive around the tip of the lake, so relaxation was put on hold. At 9.00 p.m. twelve hours after getting into the first 4x4 in Mwanza we drew up outside the Imperial Hotel.

Through the glass doors I could see David Hipkin, the head of the Kenyan branch, sitting on the edge of his chair, staring out into the night. On seeing us he rushed out, clearly greatly relieved. The pavement lurched beneath my feet as I staggered from the car and I had great difficulty in keeping my balance, for the twelve hour journey on mostly unmade roads had taken its toll on us all. As we checked in David told us how he'd thought we'd gone missing, perhaps even abducted, and had made plans to fly to Dar the following day, to try and retrace our steps. He'd then rung the offices in Nairobi, Kampala and London alerting them to our disappearance. As a consequence the whole of the company was now in a state of anxiety, believing we'd been kidnapped. Wasn't it Andy

Warhol who said everybody enjoys fifteen minutes of fame? That must have been ours.

We climbed wearily up to our room which was dark and depressing, with an over-active air-conditioner which had turned the room into a fridge. Despite our request for two beds (we knew from experience how small the doubles were) we were shown into a double- bedded room, which lived up to expectation. After pleading with the baggage boy we were shown to a twin- bedded room down the corridor. It was equally miserable. I abandoned all my plans for a long hot bath, for not only was I too exhausted but the bathroom was not exactly inviting being cold, dirty and lit by a single bulb. Instead we had a quick wash and hairbrush to get rid of some of the dust and then went straight down into the now empty dining room. I was past caring about dusty and crumpled clothes.

Once outside our room, it was hot and humid but we found a table in the dining room by an open window and the pleasant night breeze blowing off the lake helped restore our humour. Julius had gone to bed, no doubt exhausted after a day of worry and the night drive home. David H had already eaten, and so the three of us, David, Taju and I chose tilapia and chips from a not very extensive menu. At least we knew that the fish had been freshly caught that morning from the lake. It brought back happy memories of the years in Nigeria and Ghana when I would serve Niger Perch or Tilapia with **hollandaise curry sauce***.

Soon we were in bed, huddled beneath the thin grey blankets and slept well once the bed stopped moving. We were woken occasionally by the noisy air-conditioner which had a habit of switching on and off very loudly.

The next morning David had an upset stomach and dosed himself with pills for another long day in the car. Ahead lay the journey to Busia, the Ugandan border post where we would be met by Andy, then on to Kampala, the country's capital, where we would pick up Clara his wife, and then we were to head northwards up country towards the Victoria Nile.

After a hot shower we went down for breakfast. Neither of us dare have too much to eat or drink, for we knew pit stops would be few and far between. My bladder is a family joke so I was more than a little anxious. I hoped we were picking up Clara from home or an hotel, which would be a great relief – in more ways than one. After half a cup of lemon tea, I walked outside and wandered down the road, watching the early morning workers walk, cycle or travel by matatu – the local overloaded taxis – to work.

Everyone was so friendly, smiling and calling out 'Jambo, mama'. Good morning! Kisumu is very like West Africa with its small workshops lining litter strewn roadsides. Car repairs, furniture building, metal bashing and food selling are all carried out side by side whilst goats and stray dogs rummage among the rubbish. I loved the buzz, the ripe and steamy smells, the haze of diesel fumes and the brilliance of the bougainvillaea. The wide empty plains of East Africa seemed so far away, and for a few moments I felt myself once again back on the busy streets Nigeria and Ghana where my long love affair with Africa had begun.

By 8.00 a.m. we were once again on the road, having said a final goodbye to Taju who was heading back to Nairobi by car and then by plane to Dar. It was strange to think that we would probably never meet again. I wondered what would become of him in the years to come. David H was coming with us to the Ugandan border where Julius would hand us over to Andy and his driver. What a sigh of relief all these managers must have breathed when they no longer had responsibility for us.

* * *

The last time I'd made the trip from Kisumu to the border post of Busia, we had stopped just outside the town where the local fishermen had been smoking their freshly caught fish on reed platforms above smouldering charcoal fires. I remembered the stench of the fish which had been overpowering and the vultures which hovered waiting for the fishermen to turn their backs. But sadly the fishermen were no longer there. For them too, I guess life had moved on.

The journey to Busia took two hours, and was uneventful and not too bumpy. But I knew it was the lull before the storm. As we neared the border the road became blocked with hundreds of people, some in old cars and lorries, many on foot carrying huge bundles on their heads. But the majority seemed to be on bicycles. Many of the bikes were used as taxis, festooned with flags and badges and pedalled furiously by young men, whilst their passengers clung precariously with their goods on the back. Frontier posts in Africa are always mayhem, but I always enjoy them despite constantly being hassled by trinket sellers and money dealers.

We said our temporary goodbye to David H whom we would see again in Nairobi, and a final farewell to Julius who would return to Kisumu. Julius was a character - a rogue who was not without charm. When he'd visited England I had taken him out for the day to Blenheim Palace which he'd loved. He'd insisted on having his photograph taken outside the main door, arms wide open, a huge proprietorial grin on his face. I often wondered what he'd told his colleagues about the ownership of the Palace.

As soon as we got through immigration I saw Andy waiting for us. You could pick him out from the hundreds of hopeful travellers. Despite the heat, humidity and dust, he wore a formal lounge suit and tie - no doubt he felt that he had to be suitably attired when greeting the boss and his wife. Needless to say, David and I were in shorts and old shoes. What must he have made of us?

Once again our bags were loaded into the back of his 4x4 and we set off for Kampala, driven by Denis the company driver whom I'd never met. Denis turned out to be a dreadful and erratic driver and I thought grimly of the days that lay ahead. Thankfully when we were doing the last leg in Kenya we would have our old friend and driver Simon to take us around.

Kampala lay about two and half hours away and we stopped only once to buy a jackfruit and bananas from a roadside stall. Although I had often seen jackfruit, which resembles a spiky prize-winning marrow, I'd never tasted it. The idea was that we would cut it open and eat it later that day. In the event we carted it around until it went bad, and then dumped it in the bedroom bin at the Sheraton in Kampala. So I still don't know what it tastes like.

We finally came to Jinja, where the Nile starts its journey out of Lake Victoria. When Speke first set eyes on Mwanza at the southern end of Lake Victoria, the undiscovered Jinja must then have been a small fishing village. But at the turn of the 20th century it became a busy trading post and finally turned into an industrial city in the 1950's with the building of the hydro-electric power station at Owen Falls. As we drove across the iron bridge we watched the dredgers haul out mountains of water hyacinth which was left to rot at the water's edge. I wondered what those great explorers, Speke, Burton, Grant and Stanley would have made of this now thriving industrial centre. What a difference a hundred and fifty years can make.

We made our way carefully along the crowded roads, swerving to avoid potholes, bicycles and stray animals. Huge processing plants belched out smoke whilst the rubbish strewn roadsides were frantic with rickety food and clothes stalls. Large mamas, their heads swathed in vivid African head-ties, sat beneath the shade of bamboo roofs, enticing would be customers. Small bare bottomed children scampered on the dusty floor and scavenging dogs and goats rifled through the rubbish heaps. Perhaps some things had not changed at all.

Soon we left behind the bustling town and headed out towards Kampala, still some distance away. I had learnt that we were to pick up Clara at a roundabout and not at an hotel as I'd hoped, so I was glad I'd restricted myself to half a cup of tea. As we approached the city the roads became busier with people and traffic. New buildings were springing up and the roadsides were adorned with huge colourful advertising placards. Idi Amin's evil stamp was at last being erased and the whole city was clearly enjoying a new found prosperity.

I remembered my first visit not long after Amin had gone. As we had booked into the large hotel, Stephen who was then the company man in Uganda, told me that it had been secret police headquarters and that the bedrooms had been used as interrogation rooms. After torture the bodies had been thrown from the balconies. As we unpacked our bags I looked around the now pristine room with all its refined hotel trappings and shuddered. Lying in bed that night I had felt overwhelmed by a pervading sense of evil. I couldn't stop my mind from reliving the horrors that had been carried out. How many people had suffered and died in the very room in which I was now lying? Morning couldn't come too soon, and I hoped that I would never again stay in that hotel.

Sure enough Clara was waiting with her car and driver by the roadside. She was very smartly dressed in a navy suit, white shirt and elegant shoes. I was touched that she had taken so much trouble to dress so formally, and felt sorry for her that we were so casual in our shorts and t- shirts. It highlighted a difference in our cultures which is not always easy to appreciate. In Africa the more important and successful you become, the more you tend to display the trappings of success. In the West, it seems to me that the more successful some people become, the more indifferent they are to the opinions of others.

Clara's driver loaded their suitcases and several plastic containers into the back of our car. I saw a large bucket complete with lid, and it crossed my mind that this could be our portable loo. That was a comforting thought as we still had some hours on the road. But as we drove out of the city with Clara, David and me squashed together in the back seat, Clara hauled over the bucket from the luggage section and opened it up.

Inside were several individual containers stuffed full with our lunch. She had gone to so much trouble – plums, carrots, sandwiches and her homemade **chicken kebabs*** and **crunchy cookies.*** It was really delicious. We chatted about her children, their schooling, life in Uganda and if she missed Nigeria. She seemed to have settled well and was very enterprising, running her own small business making batik cloth for sale. A few months later after our return to England she sent me a delightful indigo table cloth and napkins which never fail to bring back wonderful memories of her and that magical journey.

15

MASINDI

Our ultimate destination was the Nile Safari Camp, which lay on the banks of the Victoria Nile, halfway between Lake Albert and the Murchison Falls. But it was too far a journey for us to make in daylight, and so we were to spend the night in Masindi.

I'd forgotten when I first looked at our itinerary that we had stayed in Masindi several years before when we had been visiting some sugar plantations. What had been so wonderful on that occasion had been seeing chimpanzees swinging from the trees as they called to one another as night fell. It was my first and, so far, last sighting of these wonderful creatures. Many times David and I had tried to visit the Mountains of the Moon to see the gorillas in Rwanda, but political unrest and wars had always prevented us.

At that time it had been a memorable experience staying in the hotel and I wondered if it had changed. Alas, it had not.

We arrived in the late afternoon and were shown to our room by a smiling old man who seemed unperturbed by the fact that it was full of someone else's belongings. When I pointed out the clothes and suitcases he smiled and nodded. I was by now feeling tired and dirty, in need of a lie down and desperate for the toilet. 'Could he please show us to the right room?' He assured us that this was definitely ours and proudly showed me the clean – heavily darned and very thin – sheets on the bed. 'Then perhaps he could remove the other luggage so that we could move in?' Ah, this was difficult, would we please wait in reception whilst he went in search of their owner.

The reception area was as horrendous as it had been on our last visit. It was still furnished with faded red velvet armchairs, worn bare on their arms, the springs in the seats no longer sprung. Generations of dusty and greasy heads had left dark patches on their backs. A mustard coloured vinyl sofa, split to reveal its innards, supported several ruched satin cushions. It was, as Kenny Everett would have said, 'in the best possible taste.' Its one claim to fame was that Ernest Hemingway stayed there in the 1930's after his plane had crashed near the Murchison Falls.

The hotel was a relic of colonial days having been built in 1923 by The East Africa Railways & Harbours Company. At that time Masindi was the gateway to the 'hinterland of Africa', and goods and produce from Northern Congo and Southern Sudan were shipped across Lake Albert, trucked to Masindi and then on to Lake Kyoga, finally being shipped down to Mombasa and then to Europe.

It was a long low single-storey wooden hotel with large verandahs running around the L-shaped building. At the time of our visit its verandahs were collapsing, the paint peeling, the ceilings holed with dry rot. Bare electric wires festooned the unwashed walls like forgotten Christmas garlands. But it was the only hotel in town and at the time was owned by the government. I understand that it has now been privatized and is in the throes of modernization. I don't suppose I shall ever see it again but its memories will stay with me for ever. I even feel a little sad to think that it will become just another bland and universal hotel.

The dining room doors were opened to reveal a nurses' convention in full swing. Gales of giggles and waves of loud voices swept over us. I could make out various charts pinned on the walls and redundant notes from the morning's lectures were scattered on the floor. No doubt the suitcase owner was in there somewhere. By now my bladder was in urgent need of relief and I was glad when we could finally take over our bedroom. And 'our room' it was, for this very room, number 7, was the one we had slept in on our last visit. It had not changed, except that it was even dirtier and more run-down. It is difficult for anyone who has not been to Africa to appreciate just how bad, bad can be.

Room 7 was at the end of the verandah. Inside the walls and woodwork had all been painted – in the distant past -　a deep blue colour that is found for some reason, all over Africa. No-one seemed to have considered washing off the dirty finger marks which were compounded by water streaks where the rain had come in through the leaking roof. The high ceiling bore gaping wounds where the wooden slats had rotted over the years. A solitary 40 watt bulb dangled from a brown plaited flex. Maybe we were better off without the glow from a 100 watt which would have only highlighted the squalor. We could forget all thoughts of reading in bed.

The bathroom was interesting. There was no lid on the cistern, no seat on the toilet, and no water anywhere. Well, no running water – there was water in a large yellow plastic oil drum which stood about four feet tall, was incredibly heavy and was wedged between the bath and the toilet. But to give the hotel its due we had been supplied with a round red plastic washing-up bowl. By carefully tilting the oil drum – it took two of us to do it - we could manage to fill the bowl for flushing and washing.

Bathing was clearly out of the question but with a bit of ingenuity I managed to stand in the bath and tip a bowl full of cold water over me for a quick all- over wash. Using the water for teeth cleaning though was not a good idea and I had to rummage in our bags to find half a bottle of mineral water. I closed my eyes as I brushed my teeth, for the washbowl was crazily paved with brown, germ-laden cracks.

Peeling back the grubby counterpane I lay on the thin clean sheets and found the bed surprisingly comfortable. We both slept for an hour and then joined Andy and Clara for a drink. We sat outside at a wonky metal table, on what had been the badminton court. The pot-holed road ran along the other side of the purple bougainvillaea hedge and we could hear the chatter of the villagers biking past, and smell the fumes of passing trucks which rumbled by belching out exhaust.

Clara was beautifully dressed in a soft grey frock and I was glad that at least I'd remembered to pack a pair of silk trousers and top. I gave her a present of a silk scarf which I'd bought for her in England. I think she was pleased with it.

As we chatted and watched the light fade, hundreds of bats flew above us, sweeping about the jacaranda and flame trees. On the telegraph wires the swallows chattered, pausing on their long flight back to Europe. Who knows but perhaps they were on their way to France and the house which was, as yet, unknown to us? Dogs howled in the distance and children shouted and laughed as the frogs began their evening courtship. As I drank my G&T half listening to the conversation, half drifting away, I thought just how lucky I had been to have shared with David the horrors and the beauties that are Africa.

Our dinner table was laid outside, for the nurses were still in charge of the dining room. As we settled down to study the menu, we were amazed to see about ten middle-aged and elderly Europeans turn up with their English guide. Listening to them I discovered that most of them had lived in Uganda as children. How different it must seem to them now, how shocking the contrast. One talked of going to school in Nairobi, whilst another who arrived late for dinner explained that she'd just been for a walk to see her old house. I have mixed feeling about going back. I understand our fascination to re-live the past, especially when it is longer than our future, but distance lends a much needed enchantment and once our illusions are shattered they can never be mended. Our memories are in many ways our security blanket, lulling us into a sense of timeless permanence. We relinquish them at our peril.

The dinner was surprisingly good – goat stew with rice - considering the enormous difficulties under which the staff worked, and all of them were so friendly and helpful. But by ten o'clock we were all tired for it had been a long day and so wandered back to our rooms. We found they'd been sprayed, which was just as well, for the mosquito nets were non-existent and the mesh at the windows had holes large enough to let in the bats. So as an extra precaution we both sprayed ourselves again with mosquito repellent and took our daily anti-malarial pill.

As I drifted off to sleep I thought of the life we were leaving behind, of the old friends we would probably never see again and wondered what new experiences and friendships lay ahead in the coming years. Did our future lie back in England or would we realize our long held dream of life in France? Then I fell into a deep sleep, my battered body too exhausted by days of travel to take heed of the squalor of the room or the strange shriekings of the night.

16

THE VICTORIA NILE

I woke the next morning to find it still dark. But dawn comes suddenly in Africa, about 6.00 a.m. and with it the sounds of chattering birds and a waking township. The thought of another day squashed into the back of the car with Clara's ample thighs pressed against mine, was not a happy one. But I soon dismissed the difficulties and concentrated on the possibilities of the journey ahead. From now on the territory would be completely new to me and I was keen to get on the road and finally see the Victoria Nile.

At 7.30 a.m. we set off again, our bags now full of dirty washing. I was hoping that we would be able to get some washing done at the camp, as the clothing situation was becoming desperate. It would be several days, in fact not until we stopped in Nairobi where we were to spend two nights, that we would be able to hand our clothes over to the laundry.

As we headed north, the dirt roads became more rutted and hazardous. The car frequently leant at alarming angles as a wheel dropped into a deep trench, gouged out by the tropical rains. Because the air-conditioning had now failed we were forced to open the windows. The result was that we and our luggage were covered in thick dust. The landscape appeared untamed and uninhabited. The rich red laterite soil stretched as far as the eye could see, fading into the hazy blue of the distant hills. Then suddenly out of nowhere a small hut would appear, the earth around it trodden hard and shiny, with thin- limbed children squatting in the dirt. Small cassava and maize plots were carefully tended to provide the important staples of their diet. To this no doubt would be added goat meat and fish, fruit and berries. As we neared the river the vegetation grew more lush, the exotic Borassus palms dotting the ridges and the valleys in between .

A rusty signpost leaning at a bizarre angle indicated that the Murchison Falls Park – also known as the Kabalega Falls National Park – lay ahead. I'm always reluctant to use the word 'park' because of its European connotations. But in Africa the word simply implies a designated area which is protected from human habitation and domestic animals. The Murchison Falls Park covers an area of 3,840 sq km, and had been described by Winston Churchill, as 'Kew Gardens and London Zoo rolled into one'. Once home to millions of animals the park had been ravaged by recent wars and poachers, leaving a landscape deeply scarred. But slowly the animals were returning and new hotels were being built to attract Uganda's burgeoning tourist market.

We drew up to a barrier where we had to stop and pay our fees to enter the area. A small village of maybe eight huts had grown up around it and we clambered out of the car, glad to stretch our legs. We walked over towards the guard smartly dressed in his army fatigues. Whilst Andy produced the necessary paper work and David sorted out the map, I wandered around talking to the children who played beneath the paw-paw trees, groaning with fruit. Their mother was brushing the sun-baked earth with a bundle of twigs, and in another hut a young woman stirred a pot suspended over a small open fire, which filled the hut with choking smoke.

Back in the car we decided that we should first visit the Falls before looking for the camp. The track was narrow, tortuous and deeply rutted. I wondered how deliveries were made to the camp, and if perhaps they had to come by river. The path opened out eventually into a wide clearing, in the centre of which was a huge tree. Beneath were empty wooden benches, offering cool and shade. A friendly guard emerged from a small hut and offered to take us down to the falls.

As we emerged from the shade into the penetrating sunlight, I became aware of dozens of tsetse flies which swarmed about us. The next moment I felt a sharp jab in my arm and for the next few days my arm would be red, swollen and painful. David didn't appear to notice the bite on his leg, but it gave him problems for several days, when he could no longer do up his shoe.

We clambered over the wet rocks until we stood above the 7 metre fissure through which the Nile exploded, cascading with deafening intensity down a 40 metre drop into the seething cauldron below. A fine spray rose high into the air from the white foaming falls, and imprisoned by the sunlight, painted a myriad of rainbows.

 Far below us as the river emerged from its turbulent depths, it slowed, widened and then meandered sedately on its journey towards Lake Albert. It was both terrifying and mesmerizing. A narrow tortuous track led down the edge of the cliff face, through the lush undergrowth to the foot of the falls. But Clara's tottering heels ruled that journey out. I can't say I was too disappointed as the climb back in the heat would have been tough.

Before setting off in search of the camp we sat for a time under the shade of the tree and ate an apple, the last of yesterday's lunch. Was it really only in 1864 that Samuel Baker and Florence - later to become his second wife - had been the first European explorers to marvel at the magnificence of the falls?

In 1859 the widowed Samuel, it is said, had met the 15-year-old Florence in a harem in Bucharest, where she had been kept since being captured by slave traders as a small child, after the murder of her father. Baker secured her release and took her with him as his companion. Together they had set off to Africa, to try to settle the issue of the source of the Nile. It was only later in 1865 when they returned to London to much acclaim, that they married.

He and Florence had traveled for months, endured unbelievable hardships, and had come close to losing their lives many times. What must they have thought when they finally rounded the bend in the river and saw before them 'the greatest waterfall of the Nile'? Baker had named it in honour of the then President of the Geographical Society, Sir Roderick Murchison. How ridiculously easy our own journey had been in comparison.

17

PARADISE ON THE NILE

Nothing stirred in the landscape. The mid-day sun was burning in a cloudless azure sky, and the dry baked earth sprouted sparse golden grass. Small plots of cassava struggled for survival where villagers had scratched out the undergrowth to create their smallholdings, known as *shambas*. Since setting off early that morning we had seen surprisingly little wildlife, only the kob, a large antelope which I'd never seen before on any of my travels.

Then unexpectedly, the camp was before us, perched on the banks of the Victoria Nile. We drew up alongside another 4x4 and a smiling Ugandan wearing a white t-shirt and shorts, came over to help with our bags. I was really surprised when the manager came out of the round thatched hut which was his office, to discover that he was a white South African. Maybe the standards here would be higher than last night in Masindi, for I knew that the South Africans were hard task masters. I was not disappointed.

Carl showed us to our tent which was built on a wooden platform jutting out over the dense undergrowth of the river bank. A sitting area with two deep chairs and a table created a wonderful private viewing deck. Inside were two beds brightly covered with African print counterpanes, bedside lights which worked courtesy of the generator until midnight, a small set of shelves and a table bearing a thermos flask of drinking water, mosquito coils, matches and candles. The Bakers would have been very comfortable here. The 'bathroom' was a real treat, with running water and a flush toilet. The shower cubicle, which was built outside the tent was made of bamboo slats with an overhead bucket shower. I discovered the 'walls' didn't hide very much from anyone who happened to be walking past. But then safaris are not for the bashful and feint-hearted.

I asked Carl if there was any chance of getting some laundry done? No problem, just tip it all on the floor and it would be taken care of. Such luxury! After years of picking up dirty clothes from teenagers' bedroom floors, I could finally turn the tables. I dumped everything in a grubby heap and then wandered outside for a stroll around the camp before lunch.

The Victoria Nile was a huge slow moving river at this point, where vast islands of reed beds provided cover for thousands of birds, and in whose depths the hippos whiled away the daylight hours. The camp had six tents, six log cabins and could cater for a maximum of twenty-four guests. That day we appeared to be the only visitors, although about ten Germans were holding a day workshop there. It was the German authorities, the G.D.C. who had been employed to manage the park and to try to restore it to its pre-war glories. Without their help I think the Ugandan Government would have had a difficult struggle on its hands.

The German party were lunching around the outdoor Tamarind Bar, whilst we were given a small table in the round thatched dining hut. Sitting at the table with its red check cloth, we could gaze out at the silent slate-grey waters of the Nile. Carl wandered over and suggested that after lunch we might like to do the boat trip to the bottom of the falls, as the Bakers had done, on their journey of discovery. Then he strolled across to chat to the German contingent. There was only one woman in the group. She was in her thirties, with a strong bony face which was quite masculine it is structure, but softened by cascades of dark wavy hair, falling down her back. Carl slid his hand down her spine and gently squeezed each buttock.

Lunch was delicious. Minestrone soup followed by cold meats and salad. I was surprised to learn that everything was delivered by road and not by river. It must be very difficult in the rainy season when the tracks are running with water, their surface washed away. We lingered over coffee and occasionally a gentle breeze wafted in from the river and through the open sides of the hut. The light outside was brilliant, forcing me to wrinkle up my eyes as I scanned the horizon. But it is this excess of light and colour, of sounds and smells that makes Africa so entrancing.

During lunch I'd thought nervously about the boat trip, hoping that the boat would be a decent size. There was no way I was going to paddle a canoe down this river which was seething with hippos and crocodiles. I shuddered as I recalled with horror the trip we'd made in the Okavango Delta in Botswana, some years before.

Having spent some time in the Kalahari Desert, we had moved on to the Okavango Delta, where we had planned, among other things to explore the waterways. It takes four months for the flood waters of the Okavango, which rise in Angola, to reach the Delta – the largest inland Delta in the world covering an area of some 15,000sq.km. When we were there the waters had just started to arrive and you could see the dark brown and green channels slowly filling up. Some channels were narrow streams, others wide and full waterways, all of them heaving with hippos and crocodiles.

I'm the first to admit that I'm not physically brave. I find water and small boats frightening. I find water, small boats and crocodiles terrifying. A trip through the waterways had been planned for us in a tiny native dug-out canoe called a makoro. We'd been given clear instructions before we got in not to move and above all not to try and balance the canoe if we felt it tipping. We were to leave it to the experienced guide who with his long pole would stand at the rear and push the boat along. 'Imagine that you're a sack of potatoes' we were ordered. David and I climbed gingerly in. The canoe wobbled furiously as we lowered ourselves onto the tiny wooden planks which served as seats. We cleared the river level by about six inches.

It was amazing what terror could do. There had been no problem pretending to be a sack of potatoes, I had become one quite easily. For the first ten minutes I concentrated hard on breathing as lightly as possible so as not to disturb the balance of the canoe. I was aware of the poler standing just behind me, his bare feet straddling the boat, his body bending towards the water as he silently pushed the pole into the river bed.

I forced myself to look into the channel. It was the colour of Earl Grey tea. The stems of the water lilies danced below the surface, swaying seductively in the shimmering light. The channels were so narrow that we were often forced to part the tall reeds with our hands. After a while I began to relax. It was all so wonderful. The bird life was magical, the grasses and lilies exquisite, the silence as we drifted along, idyllic. Our two friends Roger and Heather were in the canoe in front, and from time to time the polers would whisper urgently to one another, pointing ominously ahead. My heart would begin to beat fiercely - did this mean a man-eating croc had been about to attack or had we been about to hit a submerged hippo?

I'd force myself to take a few deep breaths and would try to convince myself that the polers were experts and there was absolutely, but absolutely, nothing to worry about. Not much different from punting on the River Cam really!

Suddenly there was an urgent whisper, a jabbing finger indicated that we'd at last found a large pod of hippos. We steadied the canoes in front of a large reed-edged pool, at the far end of which we could make out about six or eight hippos. Our polers inched forward. I was more than happy to stay where we were. We had been seen. One or two of the hippos sent out warning yawns and bellows. Then one hippo made a threatening charge and we made a hasty retreat. But then to my horror the polers decided to go in again. The hippo had had enough. He rushed at us with ferocious speed. Our polers realized then that they'd better move quickly, and so we retreated as fast as possible with the irate hippo gaining ground and Heather shouting 'Do something Roger!' I could almost feel the hippo's breath on my back. I can honestly say I have never been so frightened in all my life.

Later we'd been told how a South African woman had lost her life there a few months previously, when a hippo had overturned the boat and attacked her. If I'd known that beforehand...........

But maybe the Nile boat would be more than a canoe. It was not due until 2.30 p.m. so we had half an hour sitting outside our tent with field glasses scanning the river, the banks and the distant islands. Even from this distance I could see hundreds of hippos and huge crocodiles basking on the banks, just waiting to challenge the foolish explorer.

The great slow- moving waters of the Victoria Nile, like a swathe of silver ribbon, drifted effortlessly toward Lake Albert. Patches of water hyacinth floated innocently past, their destructive core hidden beneath exquisite lilac-coloured flowers. Hippo snouts would suddenly puncture the river's surface with great splashings and bellows as I sat deep in my chair, sheltered by the overhanging trees, lulled by the motionless heat of the afternoon.

Suddenly the boat appeared, chugging towards the landing stage. It looked large enough not to be overturned, and was built to take quite a few passengers who could have a decent seat well above the river level. A wave of relief swept through me, now I could look forward to the journey. Taking my bag with sunhat, sun-cream, binoculars and camera, I picked my way carefully down the rocky path towards the tiny wooden landing pier. Carl had supplied us with soft drinks, for we would be away for over four hours. The Germans joined us but they were only going as far as Paara where they were based, a few kilometers upstream.

We set off towards the Murchison Falls, sheltered from the scorching sun by a canopied roof. On the far side of the river, which was more than half- a- mile wide, waterbuck grazed at the water's edge. The vegetation was thick and lush, and amongst the reeds and rushes I could see an amazing number of birds. There were at least three hundred different species in the Park and I was lucky if I could identify twenty. But even I could recognize the European swallows as they swept the skies in search of insects. Very soon they would be starting their long journey back home, and maybe even returning to our Lakeland barns. What stories we would be able to share.

We drew in to the south bank to let off the German group and waited for about ten minutes silently swaying in the afternoon heat. Then we were joined by a few locals, either staff or their families who were joining us for the afternoon trip.

Our Captain was Francis who had sailed this boat for over thirty years. He must have lived through terrifying times, and as I watched him puffing gently on his pipe it was impossible to imagine that this slender quiet man could ever have lived through years of such violence and depravity. Yet how resilient we humans are, how soon we forget.

A young pregnant woman with a striking profile and elegantly plaited hair collected our money and was to act as our guide. We pulled away from the bank and drifted out into the Nile, heading upstream towards to falls. The sight of so many huge crocodiles basking at the water's edge was breathtaking. I had never seen so many altogether, or seen such huge specimens. Some were at least 5 metres long, with huge girths, as if they'd swallowed a hippo. Many lay with mouths agape, cooling off in the heat of the afternoon. This was not the place to fall in. Usually a crocodile will slip into the water as you approach but these refused to budge. Francis explained that they were guarding eggs and so would stay with them.

As we slowly chugged upstream our young guide and Francis would disagree from time to time over the identification of a bird and then a battered copy of **Birds of East Africa** would come out and be defiantly thumbed through. Suddenly Francis turned off the engine and we drifted silently towards a small island of reeds. Quietly but excitedly he pointed to a solitary shoebill stork. This tall grey stork with his huge comical bill is also known as the whale-headed stork and is found specifically in this area of Uganda and is extremely rare. We were incredibly lucky to have seen it and were told of an American visitor who had offered his guide $100 if he could get to see one. I gather he never did. Imagine our delighted gloating when we saw a second one the following day.

There was no shortage of hippos. Every few yards we saw another pod, and despite the heat some were out of the water grazing on the luxuriant vegetation. How huge they are when you see them on land, and how I shuddered when I remembered the canoe chase in Botswana. Looking at them from the safety of this boat was really quite a pleasurable experience.

The sound of the falls reached us long before we saw it. The river now flowed more urgently, its surface splattered with blobs of brown foam, whipped up by the sheer force of the cascading waters. We rounded a bend and there before us the awesome falls thundered hundreds of feet into a cauldron of deafening white water. It was both wonderful and terrifying. But what must the Bakers have felt when after all those years of struggle and deprivation, pain and desperation they had found themselves being tossed wildly about in their canoe at the will of this great force of nature?

I saw a figure standing on the bank and Francis edged the boat forward until our guide from the morning's walk – for that's who it was – could be handed a package from the boat. It was probably his clean laundry. Then Francis manoeuvred the boat to a small rocky outcrop in the middle of the river from which we could see the full beauty of the falls. It was possible to clamber out of the boat and onto the rocks but one slip……. So I stayed in my seat whilst David of course couldn't resist the challenge. I handed him the camera and turned away as widowhood flashed before my eyes.

Now it was time to start our journey back downstream, this time going with the current of the river. We didn't stop for sightseeing anymore but gently chugged along as the sun began to sink and spread its crimson fingers along the horizon. Above us the swallows swooped wildly feeding off the shimmering mass of insects which filled the evening sky, fuelling themselves for their long journey north.

At Paara we said goodbye to our pregnant guide and the handful of passengers who all left the boat to return to their village. Only the four of us remained. No-one spoke for the final part of the journey. I think each of us had been deeply moved by everything we had seen that afternoon and I at least needed to savour the sights and smells, to imprint it all deep in my memory, for I knew that, unlike the swallows, I would never return. Tomorrow we would head back to the city and begin the final stage of our goodbye to Africa.

As the camp came into sight the day finally fled away, leaving the river running with the blood of the dying sun.

18

GOODBYE TO PARADISE

We stepped ashore leaving the falls far behind us, said goodbye to Francis and made our way up the steep bank to the camp, which was now lit by hanging lanterns – darkness having already arrived. Suicidal moths flung themselves against the flickering lights and all around us the air was filled with the strange cacophony of an African night.

But before dinner and our longed-for G&T, it was time for a shower and change of clothes. Balancing painfully on the pebble floor, we shared a bucket of hot water and then clean and refreshed we picked our way along the dark paths, towards the makeshift bar.

Because it was Friday, four more visitors had arrived for the weekend. We paused to exchange a few pleasantries and then Andy and Clara joined us and we wandered over to a table and four chairs which were placed beneath a huge floodlit tree overlooking the Nile. Swinging from one of its sturdy branches was a large hooded wicker chair – so large that I could lie back on its deep cushioned seat and gently sway, whilst my half drunk G&T slurped dangerously in the glass.

Suddenly all the lights went out – the floodlight had overloaded the generator. Soon the rest of the lights were restored but our tree stayed in darkness. Now I could lie back and watch a million stars dance amongst its leaves. Below us the river ran silently - save for the occasional hippo bellow - as the moon floated and shimmered on its silver surface. In the far distance I could hear the roar of lonely lion. It was one of those rare and magical moments when 'all was right with the world' – a memory never to be forgotten. How vividly it comes back to me now when I lie on my back in my French garden staring up at the shooting stars on a hot summer's night listening to the call of the barn owl or the cry of a fox deep in the woods.

Our dinner table had been laid at the end of a wooden pier, jutting out over the river. The other diners were seated far away beyond the bar and the camp fire. So we sat in solitary splendour, lit by candles burning in mediaeval-style iron candlesticks. At each corner of the pier huge rolls of tightly packed paper, soaked in kerosene, blazed fiercely from tall metal poles. I was so overwhelmed by the atmosphere I can't remember at all what we ate but it really didn't matter. In that setting, peanut butter sandwiches would have tasted like *haute cuisine*.

Later, returning to our tent in a haze of exhaustion and red wine we found the heat inside it overwhelming. So we left open the flaps, closing only the mosquito netting which would hopefully deter any curious night-time visitors. At first I needed only the sheet, but later a cool wind blew in from the river and I huddled, shivering, beneath the blanket.

That night the hippos were very close by and I could hear them crashing through the undergrowth on the embankment below the tent. Then suddenly I was aware of a very strange noise which came from just outside the tent. I tried to commit the sound to memory so that I could repeat it the following morning and discover just who it was.

I couldn't help but recall with a shiver, one year in Botswana when we were camping in an even wilder place than this, that I had woken suddenly with the feeling that something had brushed my head which had been touching the side of the tent. I'd waited and listened but could hear nothing and had finally fallen asleep. The next morning when we'd walked outside, we'd discovered animal prints all around the tent. Our guide had come over 'Ah, you had five lions walking round your tent last night' he grinned. Later that morning we'd been taken on a walking safari to follow their tracks.

Armed only with a stick we were instructed that should the guide shout 'Run!' we must do so immediately - not out into the open where we could easily be caught - but head for the nearest tree and climb it! Needless to say I spent most of the walk looking for suitable climbing trees. Even the guides in Botswana were not allowed to be armed. Thankfully the lions appeared to have gone back across the river, which seemed to disappoint Joseph - but not me.

At 6.30 a.m. we were awoken by the clattering of a tea-tray as it was delivered outside the tent. Today was to be another long and arduous one, for we were to drive back to Kampala for our official farewell dinner. But first we'd decided to take the ferry from Paara and explore the country on the other side of the river. We would have only a couple of hours of exploration as we would have to set off by midday. So after a quick breakfast and having collected our packed lunches we said goodbye to the Nile Safari Camp. Carl was nowhere to be seen, no doubt tucked- up warmly comforted by happy dreams.

Denis drove us to the ferry where he would wait until our return. as we needed his place for our guard. Armed rebels and poachers were still active in the area so we had to be escorted for our safety before crossing the river. Not long after our visit I read how armed bandits had attacked a car full of tourists in Paara, killing one of them. Andy volunteered to do the driving. It proved not to be a good idea.

We waited as the ferry was winched over. ' Ferry' is perhaps too grand a word – basically it was a large decaying wooden platform with a small wheel house and engine. The idea was to drive on at one end and off at the other. However the platform was so rotten that only one end was useable, which meant that it had continually to be swung around to present the safe end to the bank.

Whilst Andy negotiated the drive on, I decided to stay out of the car and walk on board. This was a smart move as I discovered Andy's driving skills and eyesight left a lot to be desired. We were then joined by our smartly uniformed guard called George who clutched a large rifle with its end plugged with an old cork. I felt reluctant to ask if he had any bullets and just hoped the sight of him sitting up front would deter any would- be bandits. And since we never encountered any, I guess it must have done.

Perched high above the river were the remains of Queen Elizabeth Lodge. In the 60's this had been especially built for the Queen's visit but, now ravaged by war neglect and indifference, it was just another ruin. No doubt one day someone will do it up and make a fortune. We were amazed to see a huge Serova hotel complex underway complete with swimming pool, not far from the river bank. I hope that in its efforts to attract tourists that Uganda doesn't kill the goose that lays the golden egg. It is because this area is wild, untamed, untouched by so- called civilization that it is so enthralling. That's not to say that the country shouldn't strive to improve its peoples' standard of living, but these vast tracts of land should be left to the wildlife and if visitors really value it they should be prepared to do without the trappings of air-conditioned hotels and mini-bars.

For the next two hours we saw no one. Once those rolling plains teemed with wildlife but the war and consequent poaching had reduced their numbers drastically. At the time we were there only 10% of the game which originally roamed the grasslands remained. Of 14,000 elephant there were only 1,200 left. But the numbers were slowly increasing under the careful husbandry of the German team. In a strange way the decimation of the elephants had had a beneficial effect, for in the past they had almost destroyed the habitat as they stripped and uprooted the trees. Now the forests were growing back allowing the other resident animals to regain a hold. But I was disappointed that we saw so little. I suppose too many visits to the Serengeti had spoilt me. However I'm sure that in a few years time those plains will once again pulsate with wildebeest, elephant and rhinos.

It was then that we had our second sighting of the shoebill stork. We turned off the engine and watched him quietly through our binoculars. The stillness was broken only by the rustle of the grasses and the distant shriek of a fish eagle.

Then, remembering our night-time visitor I imitated it for George who immediately identified it as a hyena. Perhaps I was better off not knowing that in the night. I think they are my least favourite animal in Africa, followed closely by the baboon.

At mid-day we returned to the ferry and were winched back almost immediately. This time we all got out as Andy shunted backwards and forwards over the rotting planks. By now I think we'd all realized that driving was not one of Andy's strong points. In fact we'd been alarmed how many times he had driven straight into obstacles such as termite hills and how nervously he'd negotiated steep inclines. I was even glad when Denis took over, and that's saying something.

Just as we were about to set off David noticed that we had a flat tyre. It was just as well it happened before we left the camp and we were not stranded somewhere in the wilderness. We all got out and sat under a tree whilst Denis unloaded all the luggage to find a jack. By now David's tsetse bitten leg was very swollen and painful and because it was such a tight squeeze with all of us in the car it was difficult for him to find a comfortable position. I decided that I needed to find a loo before our 6- hour journey. I followed a sign post along a dusty track through prickly bushes and smelt the pit long before I saw it. Having seen it I decided that my usual technique – a squat behind a bush – was preferable.

Back at the car the chief game warden was talking to Andy and David. He was a tall very handsome Ugandan, dressed immaculately in long shorts and long socks, a fashion relic of the old colonial days. He advised us to go to the camp workshop and have the tyre fixed as the journey back would not be wise without a spare one. Piling back into the car we made our way to the village, where the workshop could be found.

The area was unkempt and chaotic with broken metal, old bits of rag and spilt oil streaking the ground. It was by then very hot and people lazed around in the shade. A group of small children, some carrying a baby brother or sister on their backs, laughed and chased each other across the dusty earth. We of course were of great interest. Little faces peeped from behind trees or stood shyly by the car, peering in. I got out to say hello. With great giggles they all ran away, only to reappear a few seconds later for another look.

Whilst Andy and Denis held long discussions with the eight mechanics, Clara and I decided to open our packed lunch. Such was the longing in the children's eyes as they watched us lift food to our mouths we decided that we couldn't possible eat it but must give it to them. Their need was clearly much greater than ours. We handed over the sausages and sandwiches as fairly as we could. Grabbing them the children rushed off with their goodies. A scraggy looking woman, her bony figure wrapped in a soiled piece of cloth chased after them. A few minutes later she emerged from the trees her mouth stuffed with sausages.

At last we got back on track and it was clear we'd have to drive fast if we were to make dinner. All the managers and their wives would be looking forward to a night on the town and all of them would be beautifully turned out. I thought longingly of the Sheraton bath – how I would fill it with bubbles and hot water and soak for ages. My hair would once again be clean and shining instead of stiff and sticky with dust. I did a quick time check and wondered how on earth I was going to manage a bath, hair wash and general smartening up? In hindsight it would have been better having the dinner a day later as quite clearly we were all going to be exhausted by the time we got back to the city. I hoped David wouldn't suggest we drive straight to the restaurant dressed as we were! I wouldn't have put it past him.

We'd been on the track for about half an hour when there was a great clanging. Denis stopped the car and we got out to investigate. Only David stayed inside taking the opportunity to stretch out his throbbing leg. The running board had come off at one end and was dragging on the ground. Denis looked at it for several moments. Andy chivied him and told him to undo the other end and take it off completely. Denis went through the motions of scrambling amongst the bags, looking for a tool kit. It became clear that there was no tool kit. I couldn't believe that a driver would set off on a 1,000 km journey without ensuring that he could deal with any problems.

David was not pleased to put it mildly. Andy was more tolerant. I leant against the car, which was red-hot in the afternoon sun. Looking around me I could see nothing but a sea of dried grasses and shrivelled bushes. In the distance, the shimmering hills were spotted with bushes and rocks. The sky was cloudless and the silence overwhelming. Someone made a decision to tie up the broken board and Denis managed to find a strip of rag which clearly wasn't going to last long. However, it seemed to work for the present and we set off once again. The dinner seemed to be fading fast.

We had only gone another 10 km when the running board once again crashed to the ground. This time Clara decided that she could find something more suitable and after rummaging through her suitcase she produced a large cotton scarf. I was relieved to see it wasn't the silk one I'd just given her. As we bumped along towards Masindi Andy decided we must stop there and find a mechanic to fix it as it was clear that we could not get back to Kampala without constant breakdowns. The longed-for bath was now turning into a quick shower.

Denis dropped us off at the hotel. As we walked in the waiter's face lit up with a big smile – he was genuinely pleased to see us again. The awfulness of the place was made bearable by the warmth and friendliness of the staff. How can they know that by our standards the conditions were appalling, when they live permanently in even more abject squalor? We take so much for granted in the western world.

We sat outside with a soda water and waited for Denis to return. We watched the jacaranda blossoms float to the floor, listened to the staff squabbling in their quarters. It was four before we finally drove out of Masindi, the welding completed. Andy was anxious that we were not too long on the road in the dark because of local bandits.

The last time I was there, visiting the sugar plantations, I was told about their manager who had been held up at gunpoint, stripped of all his clothes and abandoned by the roadside. I tried to imagine being left stark naked with Andy, Clara and Denis. It was not a happy thought.

19

RETURN TO THE HIGH LIFE

And so that late Saturday afternoon, we left behind the wonders of the African wilderness, the majesty of the Nile, and headed south towards the bustling and booming city of Kampala. It was Iddeh el Fittri, the end of Ramadan and the whole Muslim world was celebrating. As we drew nearer to the city we passed through small towns where everyone was out, dressed in their finest clothes. The men in spotless white gowns, their heads covered by small white 'pill boxes' often beautifully embroidered. The women were robed more colourfully, brilliant cloths elegantly draped over their heads and masking their faces. Small stalls shimmered with candles, and cooking pots and kebabs sizzled on the roadside fires. There was such a tremendous vibrancy and excitement in the air that I longed to stop the car and join in. It was much more tempting than the thought of the formal company dinner.

At 7.15 p.m. we screeched up to the door of the Sheraton, and dusty and windswept, staggered into the smart foyer which buzzed with well-dressed revelers. Much to my embarrassment the rotting jackfruit was loaded onto the trolley along with our squashed and grubby bags. We were to meet everyone at Haandi's the Indian Restaurant at 8.00 p.m. It would be a rush but I simply had to have that hot bath – although I knew the hair wash and blow- dry were now out of the question.

Whilst I ran the hot water I emptied my bag in search of a clean outfit. The dust had filtered down through all the layers. A good shake removed most of the dust but the creases stayed. I prayed the restaurant would be dimly lit for I knew all the wives would be in their best clothes for our farewell dinner.

Sliding down into the hot soapy water was sheer bliss. I could so easily have fallen asleep.

But duty called, so I grabbed the face-cloth and scrubbed myself all over. Even daily showers didn't seem to have removed all the ingrained dirt, and the water and face cloth turned brown. Tipping my head upside down I brushed furiously and watched the dust fall around me.

Both David and I felt in need of a drink before we set off, so with the few minutes we had to spare we rushed to the lift where I put on my lipstick and sprayed myself with perfume. Fortunately we had the lift to ourselves.

The Sheraton bar was large, but darkly lit to provide atmosphere. It suited me perfectly. The local band was setting up and at a billiard table a local lady wearing white plastic shoes with platform soles and a lurex top was dangling provocatively over the cue. Sitting on high stools around the bar other young girls sipped their drinks with bored expressions. If you are young and reasonably good-looking, prostitution is a tempting way of earning a living. There were plenty of lone young men and aid workers who had ready cash. The problem for both the buyers and sellers of course is Aids which is rampant in sub-Saharan Africa. Although today Uganda seems to be making enormous efforts to tackle the problem.

A few white males clutched cold beers and surveyed the talent. Whilst David went to the bar I sat down in the shadows. Next to me two elderly Scandanavian women in sensible sandals and flowery skirts chattered away, pausing only to greet a party of foreign aid workers who passed by.

I have to admit to having very mixed feelings about how aid money is used – whilst of course much good is achieved, nevertheless the sight of row upon row of brand new 4x4s lined up outside the best hotels across Africa whilst their owners are wining and dining inside, raises certain questions. At the same time many African political leaders are certainly stashing away billions of pounds - that rightly belong to the people - in overseas bank accounts. Money which could and should be used to pay back their countries debts. The idea that Africa's poverty can be solved by western governments in the next few years is a belief held largely by idealists and pop stars, who know little of Africa and her many corrupt ways.

Through the windows I could see the floodlit gardens and pool, where hundreds of guests swarmed around, clutching glasses filled with paper parasols and swaying to the infectious live music. The young girls all beautifully dressed in ribbons and frills and the small boys in white shirts and bow ties, rolled down the grassy banks, laughing infectiously. There had been a wedding and the dancing bridesmaids were swathed in scarlet satin with corsages of gold lurex roses. The bride tottered precariously on stiletto heels smiling shyly at her new husband, her hair straightened and backcombed in a 1960's beehive. It looked a great party.

We walked out of the hotel into a balmy and noisy night. Andy and Clara were waiting for us, resplendent in Nigerian dress. How dowdy I felt standing besides them. As we drove through Kampala towards the Equatoria Complex, I realized how much the city had changed since my first visit when it was still touched by fear and uncertainty. Inside the complex I saw Chinese, Italian and Indian restaurants in addition to Haandi's where we were heading. Laughing crowds sat at the open-air cafes sipping cold beers and soft drinks. Were we really only six hours away from the great Nile and its slumbering hippos?

Our party was already seated and after much shaking of hands I was placed between two new managers. Fortunately we didn't have to order as that had been done in advance, and soon the table was groaning with delectable Indian dishes. But despite my hunger I could scarcely eat – in the dim heat of the basement restaurant I was suddenly overwhelmed with exhaustion. I struggled to keep a conversation going with my neighbours, but it was the same old problem – they would only answer questions, never ask them. I began to feel like an investigative reporter.

The heat, the noise, my exhaustion and no doubt the wine, made me lightheaded and I found myself mentally slipping away. An enormous sadness came over me as I realized this was our final company farewell. The next day David had last meetings in the office and then he and I were to leave for a few days travelling alone up the Rift Valley in Kenya to Lakes Baringo and Bogoria. And by then we would be yesterday's people.

20

LAST KOBO

F or the final years of his working life, David had been
responsible for the dealerships of earth -moving equipment
throughout West and East Africa.   And so when the time
came for him to retire we'd traveled to Nigeria, Ghana, Kenya,
Tanzania and Uganda so that he might say his goodbyes.

During our final trip to West Africa, we had flown down to
Sapele in the Delta State of Nigeria.   We were accompanied
by Bob and Gill Clarke who were both friends and colleagues.
The reason we'd flown by small plane rather than drive was
that the roads were increasingly dangerous, and hijackings and
shootings were unfortunately all too common.

Sapele lies about 60 miles from the sea where the Benin river
divides into two branches - the Jamieson and the Ethiope. It
is a busy port and the area processes timber, rubber and palm
oil, as well as having a large manufacturing industry. Sapele
town lies on the left bank of the Ethiope river.

At that time the town was barricaded at night by armed soldiers manning the road blocks in an effort to prevent bandit raids on the local community. We were staying at the home of Christopher, the Nigerian head of the timber business. Set on the banks of the river it was a delightful old colonial house, and David and I stayed in the smaller guest house set in the lush gardens.

But my concern during that visit was not the local thugs but the agony of my tooth abscess. Not only was it incredibly painful but my face had swollen and I looked horrendous. There was no chance of a dentist until we got back to Lagos so I had to dope myself every four hours with pain killers and try to forget it.

Christopher was a delightful host and after drinks and a game of darts, we were joined at dinner by a local doctor and his wife. The doctor raised his eyebrows at the amount of salt David poured over his food and suggested he cut down. No chance.

That night I tossed and moaned and was glad when dawn broke and the birds began chattering and I could hear the swish of the garden boy's broom outside the bedroom window. The men were working that day but Christopher told Gill and me that he'd arranged lunch for us at one of the company's rest houses. A short trip by boat he told us.

The garden sloped down to the wide river and shortly after breakfast a small motor boat arrived at the jetty and Gill and

I clambered aboard. Both the launch and the 'Captain' had seen better days. But our 'Captain' was friendly and dressed in a grey (once white) uniform with frayed cuffs, a too-large hat and bare feet. We settled ourselves as comfortably as we could on the wooden bench. We set off slowly as the engine fired itself fully to life. Leaving behind the leafy bank we soon found ourselves mid-river passing on either side huge rusty tankers some of which were obviously un-seaworthy. We realized how tiny and vulnerable our little boat was. Gill and I glanced across to each other and cupping our hands around our mouths tried to have a short conversation. But the boat was now flying and the wind swept away our words. We looked at our watches and realized that we'd already been traveling for a long time. Glancing around the boat we saw there were no life jackets, nothing to eat or drink. So if we broke down......! Perhaps we were about to be abducted for ransom?

I edged forward to speak to our captain. 'How much further?' I bellowed into this ear.

'Long time' came the reply.

Eventually we turned off the main river and edged our way into a small tributary. The reason we had slowed down so much was not only because the river was suddenly so much narrower but because it was also filled with water hyacinth which meant we had to force our way through the dense weed.

On either side the forest was now thick and verdant. It was also very humid. Christopher had told us the previous evening that there were still a few pygmy elephant around. But I'm not sure if that was true. How wonderful it would have been to come across one. Instead we only passed a few dugout canoes and the occasional mud hut.

But then were shocked to suddenly see huge flames shoot above the forest top. Dragons maybe? No, only flares from the distant oil fields of course. What a bizarre contrast between past and present.

Having left Sapele after breakfast we finally arrived at our destination at lunchtime. The boat drew up to a small wooden jetty surrounded by deep forest. Gill and I clambered out – pleased to have arrived in one piece. We wondered how we were going to get back – not by boat we were told. A 4x4 would collect us after lunch and take us back in time for dinner.

Lunch was at the company rest house which I think must have been built in the 1950's. Walking down the narrow track we soon came to the small wooden bungalow surrounded by a wooden stoop. We were met by the steward who had the wonderful name of Last Kobo. The kobo is the lowest denominational coin in Nigeria, and as the baby of the family he was clearly an expensive mistake.

Inside it was dark and functional. The small windows were of louvred glass with some torn mosquito netting. There were a couple of old chintz- covered chairs which were pushed back against the grimy wall, a small bookcase containing mouldy

English paperbacks and the air was filled with a pervasive, slightly musty smell. The table was laid for two.

It was very hot and sticky and I don't think that either Gill or I had a great appetite. But Last Kobo produced for us a typically English lunch. Steak (very chewy) and chips (very soggy) followed by apple crumble and custard (very good).

Our journey home was by bumpy road in a smart 4x4. It was certainly quicker but somehow didn't quite have the charm of our morning river voyage.

How I wish I could do the trip again, this time without toothache. But today the area is too dangerous with increased kidnappings and violence. The local people have never really benefited from the oil wealth and until they do, I expect the violence will continue.

21

THE MAGICAL KALAHARI

Africa is for me a memorable collage of rivers, mountains, plains and lakes, but of all the magical places I have ever visited, the Kalahari Desert comes top of the list without a shadow of a doubt.

Drinks around a campfire in the middle of the barren Makgadigadi Pans, a relic of Africa's greatest super lake which dried up only 10,000 years ago, followed by dinner under the stars at our isolated camp was an unforgettable experience.

The Kalahari Desert makes up 70% of the land surface of Botswana but is 'desert' in name only. It is in fact an arid to semi-arid sandy area covering about 500,000 sq. km of Southern Africa. Derived from the Tswana word Kgalagadi it means 'the great thirst' and its red-brown sands are dotted here and there with open grasslands, islands of Boabab trees and the vast empty spaces of the Makgadikgadi Pans.

We had flown, with our friends Roger and Heather, from Zimbabwe to Botswana in a four- seater single- engine plane. Geraldine, our young Swiss pilot with attitude and a pronounced South African accent, chewed Biltong (dried beef) and drank coke for the whole of the journey. She clearly didn't do conversation.

We landed on a small dirt strip having flown over vast pans, most of which had completely dried out, but here and there we could make out small pools of water, which provided life to those animals who'd delayed their migration. There, waiting under an umbrella acacia was Adrian, our young guide with his open- top jeep. Having unloaded our bags and said good-bye to Geraldine we waited whilst she taxied bumpily back down the track and took off – a small silver fish against the cloudless sea-blue of the late morning sky.

Adrian was in his late twenties, or maybe a little older. His shoulder- length hair blew out behind him as we bumped and lurched along the dusty, rutted track towards the camp. After ten minutes we saw on the horizon the distinctive outline of an oasis of Ivory Palms. They get their name from the nut in the centre of their fruit which resembles ivory and which is carved by the Bushmen for jewellery. As we drew closer we could see the dark green of the tents camouflaged in the long grass. Immediately in front of the camp was a large water filled pan, which, until recent unexpected rains, had served as the runway. Now it was home to hundreds of flamingoes and avocets.

The six army- type tents faced towards the open grasslands and nestled unobtrusively in the vast landscape. They were very simple with two iron bedsteads, striped calico duvets, a small table between with matches and lamp, and another on which stood a mirror and two silver-coloured tins containing tissues. The tent was set on a concrete base, and the small sitting area outside had on it a dark-green canvas wash basin together with a hanging canvas bag with mirror and pockets for razors and toothbrushes. It was all very simple and tasteful and had clearly been designed to capture the essence of those first rugged safaris.

A small track led from the back of the tent to a toilet installed under a palm open to the skies. Hanging from the next palm tree was a canvas bucket shower which was filled every afternoon at half–past-three. Nearby was a rickety bamboo table with tiny mirror. We were told that the bucket held three minutes of water so we needed to devise a plan of action if we were to get our fair share. Eventually we got it down to a fine art . I stood under and got wet, then jumped out and soaped and shampooed whilst David jumped under and got wet. Then a quick change of places to rinse off. We usually managed to share the last few seconds.

All this was a far cry from the luxury camps of Southern and Eastern Africa, with their inclusive shower rooms and towelling robes but I thought it quite wonderful. The savage beauty of the vast empty grasslands and endless skies made my heart skip a beat. Now, sadly I learn that the camp has been updated and 'modernised'. How sad, for me its perfection lay in its simplicity.

We were the only guests for lunch and we ate chicken salad, served in huge wooden bowls, with nutty hot home-made bread. All the cooking was done on a primitive stone-built stove, but the results were delicious. Sitting beneath the acacia tree we looked out onto the recently formed lake, dotted with feeding birds. Apart from our murmurings and the cry of the yellow hornbill, the landscape was shrouded in a velvet cloak of silence.

That afternoon Adrian drove us out to explore the surrounding area, but first we were to stop and pick up our Bushman guide, Adam. (Surely not his given name?) Being a romantic I was excited at the thought of meeting him. Would he be dressed in a loin cloth, carrying a spear maybe? How I hoped so. He was in fact wearing a purple shell suit and baseball cap. (So much for dreams.) Even so, he was a wonderful tracker and between them, he and Adrian taught us so much. We chewed on grasses, licked stones, learnt the healing properties of the plants we saw and learnt to identify animal tracks in the dust.

The sparse grasslands grew sparser and we found ourselves driving in a landscape utterly devoid of any visible life. The once great Lake Makgadikgadi, covering 80,000 square kilometers and with a depth of up to 30 metres had been the largest inland sea in Africa. Now not a blade of grass, not a bleached tree stump could be seen. We stopped in the middle of an all- encompassing nothingness. In which ever direction we turned there was nothing to see but the endless salt -encrusted land which stretched unbroken as far as the eye could see until it merged into the silver blue of the late afternoon sky. It is impossible to capture in words such haunting beauty and overwhelming magic.

As I walked away from the others I scoured the ancient lake bed looking for signs that this barren land had once been inhabited. And sure enough small flint arrowheads and stone axes lay abandoned – shining black against the crusty grey salt dust. I picked some up and held them tightly in my hand. How long had it been since a bushman hunter had touched this very stone? How many hundreds, maybe thousands of years, had they lain here swept only by the winds and burned by the sun? I put them carefully back, hoping that there they would remain, my imprint on them, for a few more thousand years. My passport to immortality.

Back in the jeep we set off once again, heading even further away from the camp – towards oblivion it seemed. The light was fading. But then in the distance we could just make out the glow of what appeared to be a fire. Drawing closer we saw that not only was there a blazing camp-fire but also a table of drinks and a circle of canvas chairs. It was quite unexpected and strangely surreal. Putting on our jackets as the temperature began to fall with the sun, we got out of the jeep and helped ourselves to a drink. Taking a whisky and soda I walked away from the fire and our friends and, turning my back to the flames, watched the scarlet sun sink rapidly beneath the horizon. I could see quite clearly the gentle curve of the earth. Was this how it feels to stand on the moon, I wondered? The sky, which had been a blaze of scarlets, golds and turquoise, suddenly deepened to an intense navy and the first star became visible.

The only sounds apart from our sporadic conversation were the chink of ice in our glasses, the scrunch of a foot on the crusted lake bed, and that most extraordinary sound, silence itself. Then squatting on his haunches in the flickering light of the fire, Adrian began to talk to us, first of his life in Botswana as the child of a white hunter. He had spent much of his boyhood sleeping out under the stars, tracking the wildlife and learning about the San (Bushman) way of life. His knowledge of flora and fauna was incredible and we were completely mesmerized. By now the sky was an upturned bowl of stars. Stars, whose brilliance I'd never seen before. As I sat back in my chair and tilted my head towards the sky I saw dozens of shooting stars, a couple of satellites passing over – how incongruous they seemed – and the most vibrant Milky Way I had ever seen.

According to Bushman legend, Adrian told us, the stars had been made by a young girl of the 'early race'. She had first flung into the sky the warm wood ashes which became the Milky Way and which glowed at night, lighting the way for the people so that they could see to travel at night.

Then because she was angry with her mother for not giving her enough *'!huing'*, a perfumed root eaten by the Bushmen, she had flung some into the sky and the young roots had become white stars (the colour of stars when the sun comes out) and the old roots became the red stars (the stars which shine at night). Sitting there I could almost believe it.

It was bitterly cold by the time we reached our camp. We sat around the blazing camp-fire, listening to the crackling of the logs and watching the sparks fly upwards towards their sisters in the sky. Dinner was to be outside under the wide branches of the acacia tree. As we moved to the table and sat on our canvas chairs we were intrigued to see one of the trackers arrive with a large shovel. Moving over to the fire, he gathered up the hot embers and placed a heap beneath each of our chairs. Personal central heating. What bliss as the heat warmed our bottoms and travelled slowly up through our shivering bodies. Huddled down in our anoraks and fleeces we enjoyed a delicious and filling meal of casserole and rice in a setting which for me will never be surpassed.

How we laughed when Adrian regaled us with tales of wealthy visitors arriving in their Lear Jets and staggering out of their tents, dressed in little black dresses and the contents of their jewellery boxes. He recounted the story of a supermodel who had arrived with a photographic team for a fashion shoot. Hearing piercing screams coming from her tent everyone had rushed over in panic, only to find her grinning and saying 'Just testing'. They were not amused.

If I were only to be allowed one more visit to Africa I would without doubt choose to go back to the Kalahari. Not only had it been a journey to a strange and empty land, but it had been a journey of self discovery. I was recovering at the time from a near fatal car crash, had suffered facial disfigurement, endless operations and shattered confidence. But here in the desert I had finally came face to face with my vulnerability and inconsequentiality and, at last, found them bearable.

22

Lakes Kariba and Boringo

After the magnificence of the Kalahari desert we headed back to Zimbabwe and Lake Kariba. Whilst for me nothing could surpass the glory of the Kalahari, there's no doubt that Spurwing Island in the middle of Lake Kariba also had a special magic.

Kariba is a vast inland lake created in the 1950s. Surrounded by the mountains of Zambia and Zimbabwe it is extremely dramatic and awe-inspiring. We were there in the winter and even though the day-time temperatures were high, the trees on the mountain sides were bare and stark. In the summer it must have been lush and green.

We had flown from the mainland in a small plane, piloted by Ashley who was the only truly rude pilot we met on the whole journey. He'd bundled us into the tiny four-seater and then was told by control that he hadn't entered his flight plan. Swearing profusely he stormed off to see to the paperwork whilst we all sweltered waiting in the mid-day sun. Fortunately, the flight was only ten minutes, but ten minutes of Ashley was eleven minutes too long.

We flew over the tiny landing strip before turning around and going in to land, and as we taxied down the dirt runway we saw small children rushing from huts, pointing to the giant bird descending from the skies. From the window I saw our guide Andy waiting in his jeep. Ashley was extremely curt with Andy, annoyed that two marabou storks had wandered across the runway in front of the plane, and clearly neither cared for the other.

We set off in the jeep towards our small three tented camp. The weather was bright and clear and the huge skies and wide open spaces lifted my heart. Andy drove us to a high point where we got out for a beer. I looked across the wide grasslands which had once been under water. Evaporation, increased power supplies and drought had caused the lake level to drop, exposing not only new grazing lands but also the skeletal remains of once-drowned mopane trees.

We watched two lone elephants lumber sedately down towards the shore line to drink. Further inland, new mopane trees with their butterfly leaves were kept stunted by browsing elephants. As we drove to the motor boat (we were still not at the camp) we passed an elephant whose trunk was partially paralysed. This phenomenon only effects the elephant around Kariba and is thought to be caused by a then-unidentified toxin. Although this particular elephant managed by using his foot and trunk together, many don't and are doomed to starve to death.

Leaving the jeep at the water's edge we clambered into a small speed-boat . It was a glorious day, the water was like a mill pond, glittering with fallen sunlight. We gently manoeuvred between the half submerged dead trees before opening up the throttle and heading around the bay towards the camp.

Having reached the island and 'beached' the boat we clambered into another old jeep to carry us to the camp which was only 200 metres away. The reason for the jeep was the herd of buffalo which roamed around the island and which we could see grazing all around us. Walking through them would not have been a good idea. A couple of years previously two guests had been killed by a buffalo just outside their tent. Nowadays, two unobtrusive electric wires fenced off the tents, but even so, if the buffalo decide to stampede, two electric wires are useless.

We had just finished dinner one night – asparagus soup, chicken, pineapple and macadamia nut casserole, followed by cheese and then apple pie – and had wandered back to our tent. Suddenly there was an horrendous rushing, just like a tube train entering the station. We rushed out onto our deck and Andy shouted across to us, warning us that the buffalo had been frightened, probably by a lion, and had broken through the fence and stampeded through the centre of the camp, narrowly missing the dining tent and the staff quarters.

The next morning Andy took us out to search for the lion kill. Surrounded by hundreds of vultures, the disembowelled buffalo carcass had already been half-eaten. By the next day it had almost disappeared.

But the memories which still cling to me are of the idyllic boat rides when we gently edged our way around each inlet and bay. We were so incredibly close to the elephant and the buffalo who grazed at the water's edge, and as long as we stayed on the water they chose to ignore us. Being level with their feet gave us a whole new perspective and we realized just how enormous and powerful they were.

Winding our way in between the skeletal tree trunks which had been submerged thirty-five years before and which were now exposed by the falling waters, we photographed the fish eagles and the dramatic darter birds who spread out their huge wings to dry in the sun. Perhaps Dracula bird was more apt a name.

We saw so many crocodiles which was a little unsettling. I believe there was one crocodile for every one hundred and fifty metres of shore-line. The hippos, unused to being hunted were less aggressive than in the Okavango which was of some comfort to Heather and me.

On a small promontory we watched a large monitor lizard swallow a snake, a few inches of its tail still wriggling in a vain effort to free itself. What was so wonderful about the trip was the lack of other tourists, the silence and the magnificent views across the lake to the purple distant hills.

Each night we sat around the camp fire as the temperature fell. Looking across the lake we could see the lights of Kariba town and a string of bobbing lights on the kapendi fishing boats, strung- out like Christmas decorations. The air was filled with the most charming bell-like chimes of the reed frogs, which sounded exactly like a small breeze tinkling through Japanese wind chimes. From across the bay they were joined by the deeper croak of larger frogs. The symphony played on late into the night.

Along with our drinks we were served pre-dinner snacks. Sometimes fried kapendi (rather like whitebait) sometimes spare ribs and fried chicken wings. Andy talked of his future and the difficulties of living in Zimbabwe. He, his wife and two children lived on another part of the island with their Labrador – trained never to go into the water - which must have been so difficult for lab to resist. His wife took the children by boat to school each day in Kariba, which in stormy weather, must have been hair-raising. He told us of a group of youngsters who, advised not to go out onto the lake because of the weather, had ignored the advice. Their boat overturned and the following day only one of them was found alive clinging to a tree, no doubt traumatized for life.

Many of Andy's family had already left for South Africa and he suspected that he may follow. However ten years later when I was in Kenya talking to another guide, I discovered that Andy and his family were in Kenya and he was then working in the Mara.

I think today that the camp on Spurwing Island must no longer exist. Whether one day it will be resurrected who knows. But I'm so glad we had the privilege of visiting it before Zimbabwe reached rock-bottom.

*   *   *

Having said our final goodbyes to colleagues in Uganda, and leaving the Victoria Nile and Murchison Falls far behind, David and I set off to enjoy a welcome few days alone on another lake and now headed to Lake Baringo, which lies in the north of the Kenya.

As we came near Nakuru town we came across an accident between an overloaded bus and an overloaded lorry. The distraught passengers stood helpless by the roadside, their belongings scattered all around. Fortunately there appeared to be no injuries. The further north we got, the dustier the land became and the few leaves that remained on the roadside bushes were grey with dust, but as we drove into the town we came across a glorious avenue of jacarandas and for the first time saw them festooned with glorious lilac-blue flowers. We turned off the main road, following the signs to Baringo. The landscape was increasingly barren and volcanic – the dusty grey earth pock-marked with boulders spewn from the earth millions of years ago. Even so, a few goats and some half-starved cattle rummaged amongst the dried grasses for something to eat.

We'd been driven by Simon who'd been David's driver for many years on our trips to Kenya. He had originally been a teacher and was very political. Over the years I'd had some fascinating conversations with him about Kenya, her politicians and his own political ambitions. But he and I shared a long-standing joke. The first time we'd met he enquired after a trip 'And where now madame?'

'Home James' I'd replied jokingly, and was astonished when he answered back 'And don't spare the horses?' Not a visit went by without us playing the game. Now leaving us on the edge of the lake with a promise to return the next morning to take us to Lake Bogoria, Simon headed off to his own accommodation.

A small wooden jetty jutted out into the lake which was a murky brown. The 129 sq km lake is set amid arid plains, surrounded by volcanic ranges which stretch as far as the eye can see. It is incredibly hot. We'd booked to stay on Ol Kokwe Island, a stark rocky outcrop in the middle of the Lake where there was a tented camp as well as a small village belonging to the Njemps people. The Njemps are a unique tribe who are the only pastoral, cattle herding and fishing tribe in Kenya. The Masai, another pastoral tribe, are forbidden to eat fish.

An orange fibre-glass boat was waiting for us and we gingerly sat on the jetty lowering ourselves carefully as it rocked from side to side. We were surrounded by crocodiles basking in the shallow waters, shaded by the tall waving reeds but keenly watching and hoping for an easy meal. This was not the place to fall in. The mudflats bore the footprints of hippos, and I hoped this was not to be another Botswana horror trip. The boatman eased the boat out of the reed-lined inlet and then once in open waters let the throttle rip.

It was an exhilarating ten-minute ride. The wind tore at my hair and swept away our words. A lone flamingo, his carmine-tipped wings burnished by the golden sun, headed towards Lake Bogoria. Above him, far in the depths of the sky, a tiny plane scratched a white trail across the azure blue.

The lake was dotted with dozens of volcanic outcrops and we were heading for the largest island which from the distance appeared to be a huge pile of boulders rising steeply from the lake bed. We clambered out onto the gravel beach where we were met by a young white Kenyan girl who, taking our bags, led us up the shimmering rocky banks towards the camp.

How hot it was. I could scarcely breathe. The rocks held the day's sun and acted like giant ovens. We reached the summit, panting for air, noted the dining area and the pool and then were led down to our tent which lay some distance on the other side of the hill. We tottered over rocky steps, squeezed between boulders, avoided sharp cacti spears and eventually staggered into our tent.

After throwing our bags onto the bed and making a quick trip to the bathroom we struggled back up the steps to the dining room and tucked into a very good buffet salad. We were very tired after all our travels and headed back to our tent for our siesta. I stripped off completely and lay as still as I could, but even so the perspiration ran in rivulets along my body; despite having left the tent flaps wide open, there was not even a whisper of air. It was impossible to sleep and I despaired of it ever getting cooler.

As I lay there I recalled the awful visit, some years previously, to Lake Jipe on the border of Kenya and Tanzania, when we stayed at a run-down camp in small thatched round cottages with no mosquito netting and mosquitoes as big as horse flies. We'd had to close the windows to keep them out as there were no nets on the beds; the temperature was horrendous. We lay on our beds, exhausted, as the room became a sauna. Bugs fell on us from the thatched ceiling and frogs jumped around the room all night. In the end David got up and after a frantic chase around the room, managed to trap one in the waste bin. But what had been really awful was having to share the shower with six large frogs which climbed out of the drain and crawled up the walls. It was the shortest shower I've ever had.

I had long dreamed of visiting Lake Turkana which lay in the northern- most part of Kenya and which is even drier and hotter, but now, here on Lake Baringo, I was thinking maybe a trip to the Antarctic might be preferable. Miraculously, at precisely four o'clock a breeze got up and spread its delicious cool fingers across my skin, making me feel human once again.

At five o'clock we decided to take the 'Sundowner' trip across to a small island, locally known as 'Gibralter' – a small rock outcrop about a mile away in the middle of the lake. We were really lucky because we were the only clients that day and so had the small boat and Johnson and Ezekiel to ourselves. They'd packed up a cold box with beer and Pimms and we set off as the sun began to lose its fire. A fish-eagle swooped from a tree-top, clasped a fish in its talons and returned to feed its youngster which we could see perched high on its nest.

As we drew closer to Gibralter, Johnson pointed out a large hole on the cliff face, the home he told us of a giant owl which he claimed he could see quite clearly. But despite all our efforts David and I could see nothing. Rounding the cliff we finally landed on a small stony beach, and what I had thought to be a fallen log slid silently into the lake. I had a careful look around before I clambered out of the boat.

A narrow dusty track wound its way up through a tumble of boulders to the top. I stepped carefully to avoid the small rocks which could easily have sprained an ankle and clung firmly to my camera which bounced around my neck. Once at the top Johnson and Ezekiel busied themselves with unpacking the cold box whilst I explored the pinnacle gazing out at the still, muddy waters, the sprinkling of small islands and the distant purple mountains behind which the sun would soon set.

It was the most breathtaking view, utterly quiet save for the sudden cry of the fish- eagle and the scrunch of David's feet on the barren earth as he wandered back from his explorations. We sat entranced whilst the sun splattered the sky with a riotous palette of colour until finally all that remained was a golden ribbon which slid gently behind the mountains leaving us with the night. Across the water I could see the fire-fly flicker of newly-lit hurricane lamps guiding the way to the tents, a gentle reminder that life moves on and a new day will dawn.

The wind had now quickened and the darkened waters of the lake were choppy as we sped home. Despite the breeze we still felt hot and sticky after our adventure and, stripped down to our swimsuits, we plunged into the cold and newly chlorinated waters of the pool. It was sweet agony. The following day Simon took us to Lake Bogoria with it's sizzling geysers and colourful flamingoes before we set off back to Nairobi, the airport and home.

And so ended our final trip to Africa together. What wonderful memories we would take away with us. I thought back longingly to my first days in Africa, of the struggles and the hardships of bringing up three small children in war-torn Eastern Nigeria. I recalled the tears of frustration and loneliness I had shed as we struggled with empty shops, a garden full of bullets and grenades, the threat of armed renegade soldiers prowling the town at night, and the military curfew that kept us at home from 10.0 p.m. to 6.00 a.m.

However that had been only part of the story. For me there had also been the discovery of a new and fascinating world. We had pushed our way through overgrown forests, discovered remote villages, ridden on yam boats down the great River Niger, crawled through dark caves, collected butterflies, and attended strange and sometimes frightening local festivities. We had crossed the wide plains of East Africa, explored her lakes and deltas and been beguiled by the magic of her deserts.

Above all I thought of how I had struggled over the years to come to terms with the abject poverty and devastation of a continent constantly at war with itself. A continent that was both enthrallingly beautiful and miserably inefficient and corrupt. They were struggles I would not have missed for all the world.

Although David never returned to Africa, in the following years I was to holiday there many times, taking with me friends and family, seeing it again as if for the first time through their eyes. My passion never faltered, but a new life and new love lay ahead of us, this time in France.

23

MON AMI, JACQUES

The first time we met Jacques was the day we moved in. The huge removal lorry had scraped its way into the French hilltop hamlet, got stuck between overhanging roofs and finally with the help of locals eased its way to our front door, but in its struggle to round the narrow lane it had demolished some of Jacques' low-slung roof tiles.

I opened the door to find a beaming and friendly Jacques, one hand outstretched in greeting, the other clasping a cigarette between two powerful fingers. He blew the smoke away sideways so as not to blind me and then in rapid French explained the problem. I thought I understood but decided to call David just to confirm that I'd got the gist of things and also to decide how to handle the problem. Back in England I would have felt perfectly happy sorting out any difficulties, but suddenly, in another country, another language I felt like a child in a grown-ups' world. Here in France male chauvinism still lives on so I think Jacques thought it perfectly normal that I should have to resort to a little male support.

He insisted that we shouldn't have to pay ourselves but we must demand recompense from the removers. He seemed in no hurry to have the problem fixed however and in the end some months later when the builders were working on our house they fixed the problem for him. We paid of course. Looking back I think he was probably quite pleased to have an excuse to wander across and look us over. We were the first English people to come to live permanently in his village - not just holiday makers who disappeared with the summer sun. And so began our friendship.

Two days after moving in we needed to change the gas cylinder. Although David and our friend Peter who had helped with the move knew exactly what to do, doing it was more difficult. Neither had the strength to turn the knob. I suddenly thought of Jacques. There was no doubt that he looked pretty powerful. About 5'3, with a large belly overhanging very short legs he looked the epitome of an ageing prop forward. His hair was shaved close to his head and his clear, flirtatious blue eyes twinkled from a generous and open face.

Born and brought up in Paris he'd originally worked as a monumental mason and then as a dealer in second- hand trucks before finally opening a hunting/fishing shop in our nearby market town. But that hadn't lasted and now he pottered happily about with his hunting dog while his younger second wife worked full time in the wine industry. With hardly any effort he turned the knob easily, leaving David and Peter with slightly embarrassed grins.

A week or so later there was a knock on the door. Jacques stood there and insisted that we pick up a basket and follow him into his garden to pick some cherries. Not wanting to appear too greedy, I took with me a small container. Jacques looked at it with disgust and insisted I went back for something larger. His tree was drooping with the most delicious cherries I'd ever eaten. Deep maroon, fleshy and sweet. The tree looked rather bizarre as it was festooned with CDs dancing in the sunlight, supposedly to frighten off marauding birds. Those birds whose greed overcame their fear, came to a swift end. For many mornings we had heard the sound of shots, as Jacques sat on his verandah a cigarette between his lips seeing off the intruders with his rifle.

He was indiscriminate – magpies, jays, blackbirds and thrushes were all fair game as far as Jacques was concerned. He laughed when we told him that thrushes and blackbirds were so rare now that it was surely better to lose a few cherries? Making a circle with his thumb and fore finger and placing them against his mouth he smacked his lips loudly. Thrushes stuffed with *foie gras*, he told us with a grin, were '*impeccable!*'

Our basket full, he called for his wife Nicole, who was in the house. To be exact he clapped his hands and shouted for glasses. Nicole arrived, not seeming to mind the abrupt call.

She was a pretty woman and seemed very tolerant, but we later realized that she was more than a fair match for Jacques. Then he took us into the cellar under his house where he kept his wine. As he unlocked the door and led us in we were staggered to find ourselves in a domed cellar which ran the whole length of the house. Hundreds of bottles of wine from all around France were stacked in racks and at the end of each rack a slate recorded just what wines and what year were kept there. At the far end shelves groaned under jars of homemade *confit* and *foie gras* and an upturned wine cask acted as a table. On the wall was a licence displayed by all alcohol sellers – only looking closer we saw that this was a fake made by Jacques to amuse himself and his friends.

I thought at first that it must be a shop but soon realized that this was his private collection and passion. We discovered later that Jacques only really drinks when entertaining and that his daily tipple is expresso coffee which he consumes in large quantities either at home, in our kitchen, or in the Central Café. So what happened to all this wonderful wine? – we were to discover that before too long.

He opened a fine bottle of Cahors wine which tasted even more delicious and decadent at 10.30 in the morning. The Cahors wines can be wonderful, but it's extraordinary how it has been almost impossible to buy a good one in England. When we tried in the past we were always bitterly disappointed.

By the time we got home, none of us felt like work. But Hannah who was living with us whilst the stables were being turned into a home for her, decided that she must repay Jacques' hospitality and set out to make a **clafoutis*** with the cherries.

* * *

That September our fig tree groaned under kilos of figs. We couldn't bear to see them all going to waste so Hannah spent several weeks experimenting in her kitchen with jams and chutneys, but there's a limit to how many jars you can fill. So we had figs for starters, **figs for pudding,*** figs for snacks. One of our favourite quick lunches is **fig and ham salad.***

Hannah had so many jars of jams and chutneys that in the end she made presents of them to friends and neighbours. She even received an order from Parisian friends for a bulk buy the following year. Could this be the start of something big? The only problem was that she had invented the chutney as she went along and hadn't written down the quantities.

Nicole, popped round to tell us that she had a shock one morning when she put the chutney on her *croissant*, thinking it was yet another jam. But she told us that it was absolutely perfect with *confit de canard*. She was so delighted with the taste that she asked for lessons when the next batch was made. Hannah is going to have to do some quiet experimenting beforehand.

Early in the autumn Jacques knocked at the door.   He'd seen us admire his collection of *confits* (duck and geese preserved in their own fat, in jars) and *patés* in his cave and he asked if we would like some geese in order to make our own *confit* and *foie gras.?* Of course we would – we were passionate about food – but would the geese be dead, would we need to clean and pluck them ourselves? And what did we do with them? Since the builders were still in the stables and our own tiny kitchen yet to be demolished and rebuilt, it might be a little difficult to cope with all the preparation..

No problem, insisted Jacques with a dismissive wave of his hand. "I'll show you how to do it and you can use all my equipment" he added in his rapid Parisian French. He would telephone his good friend who bred a few geese for friends and place an order. He would see us the following week and gave us clear instructions on what preserving jars to buy, what sizes we needed and definitely but definitely not to buy those with rubber seals and clip tops.

'Why not?' I ventured to ask.

'Because they are not reliable – *a mon avis!*'   'In my opinion' is a favourite expression of Jacques, and now he is known affectionately by us all as - *'mon ami, mon avis Jacques'*

At least we can follow Jacques' French. He and Claude and Micheline, from whom we bought the house and who now live across the lane, fortunately speak understandable (well most of the time) Parisian French unlike most of the locals.

Madame T. our next door neighbour, who has lived in the village for nearly sixty years, raising six children in a small farmhouse with no water , speaks with a very strong local accent, rather like Catalan. Her first language, we were told, was Langue d'Oc and it took a few visits before I could tune in. But to this day I still find Thérèse, another farmer's wife, almost impossible to understand. I explained my problem to Jacques who told me she spoke a strong *patois* which even he found difficult. Now when I meet Thérèse in the village walking her hefty cart horses to new pastures, or pulling her little cart behind her full of dandelion leaves for her rabbits, I keep the conversation as brief as possible, nodding sagely and watching her face. When she smiles I smile, when she looks sad I try to look suitably sympathetic! One day I'll master it.

A few weeks later, Jacques arrived shortly after breakfast, with his farmer friend, the breeder of the geese. The two huge geese still had their heads and feet, but fortunately were cleaned and plucked. Laying them out on the kitchen table and after the obligatory expresso and cigarette, Gaston produced a huge knife and slit open the first bird to remove the *foie gras*. Undigested maize from the gizzard tumbled onto the floor whilst droplets of bright red blood spread over the table top before dripping on to the floor to mix with the maize. Hannah went for her camera whilst I followed instructions and passed the scales, washed the jars and mopped up the blood.

"Salt' ordered Jacques imperiously. I passed the sea salt.

'Non, non' he cried, then in his limited English, 'eets no good,' and went home to find the correct *Guerande* salt from Brittany and some mixed pepper corns. We mere women were given the job of cleaning up, turning the pepper mill and wiping the jars! So much for my plans to turn myself into an enviable competent French housewife in the space of a year. I hadn't banked on the strength of male chauvinism that still exists in France, but then French women didn't get the vote until 1945 so I suppose it's not so surprising.

The first *foie* weighed one- and- half kilos. The second was a little smaller. I tried hard not to think of the forced feeding, and concentrated on dreaming of dinners on the terrace and chilled Sauternes. The *foie gras* was carefully placed in the jars, seasoned, sealed and set aside for cooking. Meanwhile every part of the geese was carefully preserved for later use. Even the heads and feet are used by some of the older generation for making soup, but I decided that they could safely be binned. I gathered that Mme T. was partial to a good head and claw soup.

It took three days of cutting, salting, and cooking (in the end we worked in the barn on an oilcloth covered table) before the *confit* and the *foie gras* could be labeled and stored in our own *cave*. The first day the geese were carefully dissected into the breasts *(magrets)* then the legs and thighs *(cuisses)*. These would form the main meals later in the year. But nothing went to waste. The gizzard, heart, wings, and neck were carefully extricated for cooking and preserving and all the body fat cut into tiny chunks to create the fat for cooking and later storing. Then everything, including the carcasses, was laid in layers in a huge preserving pan, and each layer sprinkled with the special *Guerande* salt.

The first layer was the fat and the last the *magrets* and *cuisses*. We then had to leave it in a cool place overnight. In the meantime Hannah and I scrubbed and cleaned whilst the men celebrated with a glass of Armagnac. However we were allowed to join them once our work was done!

The next day Jacques turned up at nine carefully throwing his cigarette onto the garden path before bustling in and issuing orders. Now we had to remove all the pieces from the pan and wipe off the excess salt with kitchen paper. That done everything was replaced in the preserving pan and set on my cooker. Fortunately we had a large new stainless steel cooker with a wide central gas ring which could cope with the preserving pan. The cooker took up most of the tiny kitchen, but it had been bought in readiness for the new, as yet un-designed, kitchen which hopefully would be finished in time for the next *confit* season.

The pan bubbled and steamed for an hour-and-a-half, filling the whole house with delectable smells. The jars were washed and dried and lined up on the small table. Slowly Jacques showed us how to pack the *magrets* and the *cuisses* into the jars and then to top up with the hot fat. I was allowed to wipe the rim carefully before the seal was placed on top and the screw top turned tightly. My efforts were duly praised by Jacques, 'you ees doing very good.' Then the hearts, necks and anything large enough to be chewable were packed together. After that he lifted out with a slotted spoon all the remaining slivers of meat and edible debris. These would make the *fritons*, which are delicious when cold and chopped up in salad. The great joy of goose and duck fat is that it contains almost no cholesterol which is one of the reasons (the other being the strong tannin wines) why the heart attack rate in SW France is one of the lowest in Europe. Unfortunately it still contains rather a lot of calories.

Now all that remained were the carcasses and a great deal of goose fat. The carcasses were removed for later that evening and the fat put into jars to keep us supplied with cooking fat for the coming year.

The finished jars had now to be immersed in water and cooked for another hour- and- a- half. Jacques brought round his deep metal bucket especially made for cooking *confit*. The jars were carefully stacked, tea towels wedged between them to stop them moving, and heavy stones from the garden placed on top to keep them under water. A large gas ring was placed underneath and connected to a cylinder of butane. Fortunately all this took place in the barn otherwise I suspect we might not have had a house left. Jacques left us with strict instructions to let the jars cool in the water and then tomorrow they could be lifted out, dried, labeled and stored.

That evening the cooked carcasses made a wonderful meal served with green salad and fresh bread. Called *Les Desmoiselles de Quercy,* this was the typical evening meal for families once the *confit* making was over. Definitely a meal for family or close friends only we decided, as we picked and sucked at the bones and washed them down with a good strong Cahors wine.

24

NEW   BEGINNINGS

Our first spring in France had been all that we'd hoped for. Each morning I'd been woken by the sun pouring into the bedroom, the smell of lilac from across the lane wafting gently in through the window, someone's cockerel shrieking in the distance and nearby a cuckoo calling for a mate.

Then the builders would arrive. Lorries would bump down the lane, diggers trundle slowly past the bedroom windows, breaking up the road surface and knocking the edges off our garden walls. It was amazing that our neighbours were so uncomplaining. Cement mixers started churning and the smell of cigarettes pervaded the house. We had six months to convert the stables into a home, for all the family were coming over for Christmas, their tickets already booked. They were arriving before that, for summer too but there was no way we could house them all before Christmas so we'd have to sort out some other solution.

Once the stable conversion was completed the plan was to start on the main house in January, demolishing our kitchen and building a large farmhouse kitchen which in reality would become the centre of our home. David had decided that we'd install French TV in there, forcing us to listen and learn. In our weaker moments we could retire to the sitting room and watch our English television.

The first year was hell, worse than we expected. Whilst the stables were knocked about, the garden dug up for another septic tank, trees demolished for the terrace, we also started some internal work on our own house hoping to complete it all before work began on the kitchen. The moquette had to come off the sitting room walls and the ceiling carpet had to be covered with new plasterboard. David and a young friend decided to tackle the work themselves.

Although it didn't take too long the mess was unbelievable. The furniture had to be constantly moved and covered as the plaster dropped onto the floor below. I followed them around with brush and mop, stopping to make coffee every half an hour in the kitchen which was stuffed with excess furniture and ornaments. At the same time we had employed the local tiler to redo the bathroom, stripping out the fluffy pink carpet and retiling the walls and floors. Of course the toilet and bidet had to be lifted out onto the upstairs terrace and we were forced to use the downstairs toilet which was stuck in a small cupboard off the kitchen. This became known as the black hole of Calcutta. The walls were covered in dark green vinyl paper complete with bamboo pattern. The ceiling was dark wood strips and when you sat down your knees touched the opposite wall. Things would have to be changed.

I'm not sure why we decided to do everything all at once. I think the feeling was 'let's get the chaos over all at once rather than drag it out.' The only place to sit to escape the mess and noise in the meantime was on the bench by the lake at the bottom of the meadow. Gazing at the pink, white and red water-lilies and listening to the song of the grasshoppers and cicadas helped get life back into perspective.

Our mood was helped enormously too when we discovered that Gaston, who'd provided us with the geese for our confit, also grew his own asparagus. A quick telephone call in the morning would ensure that he'd have freshly picked white or green asparagus ready for us in the afternoon. The season is quite short so to avoid getting bored with the same recipes for a month I usually rotate the following three favourite asparagus dishes. **Asparagus roasted with country ham; asparagus with hollandaise sauce; and asparagus with chopped hard boiled eggs and melted butter.***

Unfortunately our first delightfully warm and sunny spring turned into a cool and grey summer. I'd hoped we'd left the Lake District weather behind, but clearly not. Our two Labradors Max and Lottie were constantly damp and bedraggled and bemused by all the chaos. They brought mud into the house and picked up tics which they frequently transferred to us.

My eyebrow tweezers were often used for purposes not dreamt of by their inventor.

Then one day Max became seriously ill having picked up a disease from a tic bite. We rushed him off to the vets and after several injections and a few days of worry he made a complete recovery. We had learnt the hard way the importance of monthly treatment for tics. It was one of the many things which we should have thought about but didn't. Life in a new country could be more complicated than we thought. It took a couple of years before we began to feel completely at ease with all the aspects of life abroad.

We definitely needed to be on site all the time. Despite having a brilliant architect and his building supervisor who paid weekly visits to the stables renovation, we were often able to forestall a potential problem, or make an improvement as the work began slowly to unfold. Plans were one thing, the reality often another. As the rooms took shape we could see where a small change would improve the look or efficiency of the house – and it was much cheaper to do it then than at a later stage.

What had been really difficult had been deciding on the lighting and where all the plugs, switches and radiators were to go in the new house. This had to be done before any work had started and we just had the plans to look at. We spent several afternoons with the plans spread out on the dining table trying to place imaginary furniture and kitchen equipment.

In the end we decided that we couldn't have enough plugs or switches and made sure we ended up with too many rather than too few.

After that Chouky, who was both plumber and electrician, told us we had to choose all the bathroom, shower and cloakroom furniture. Working from the plans he gave us exact measurements for the showers and corner bath. We had a great time visiting the showrooms and gave Hannah a free hand in choose what she wanted. So, shoes off, she wandered around lying in various baths, standing in different showers until she found exactly what she was looking for .

However the tensions of three forceful personalities living together began to show. There were frequent explosions of temper, tears and threats to return to UK. I often lay in bed at night, tossing and turning in a room full of boxes and surplus furniture and wondered if we'd made the right decision. Maybe it would have been easier staying back in England where we knew the ropes, had a comfortable and elegant home and our sons and their families within easy driving distance. But the reality was that the die had been cast, we had burnt our boats, spent a fortune on legal and financial advice and going back was really not an option. Sometimes that knowledge was helpful at other times it was frightening.

In the mornings though, as I looked down the meadow to the lake and woods and across the valley to the distant sunlit hills, my   confidence would return along with the certainty that one day all would be finished and a normal life resumed.

What bliss it would be to have my home back together again, to empty all the cartons and packing cases which were stored in the barn and re-discover ornaments, paintings and kitchen equipment we hadn't seen for a long time. Sometimes when I would urgently need to find some particular item I would have to spend ages fumbling in boxes, unwrapping objects that had been protected in sheets of paper then re-wrapping as I discovered it was not what I wanted. In the summer the heat in there was unbearable, in the cooler weather it was cold and draughty. Not only that, we shared it with a family of bats whose droppings were everywhere and who would flutter around our heads irritated that we had disturbed their daytime sleep.

So in the end, before either of the houses was completed, we bought and erected yards of metal shelving and unpacked everything in the barn, so that we could see immediately what we were looking for. Then it was off to the tip with a trailer full of cartons and paper and we sighed with relief as we restored some sort of order,   if only in the barn.

Three years after completion of the houses the shelving was still stacked with half of our belongings and I came to realize how profligate I had been and how, in reality, I needed so little. After years of 'acquiring' I began 'disposing'.   The simple life becomes more attractive, the older I become. Next time around I shall be a minimalist.

Meanwhile the old stables were slowly taking shape. August had arrived and our two sons, their wives and children arrived for their holidays. We managed to squeeze Julian, Lisa and their twin daughters Alice and Jessica into the main house but had to rent a gite down the lane for Hannah, Jonathan, Francesca and baby Theo. Sadly the two weeks they were with us the weather was disappointing, some days warm and sunny but others overcast and cool – 'it's not like this normally' our neighbours assured us, as the rain steadily fell.

We had bought a huge garden table and chairs for around the pool, but there were days when it was too cool and damp to eat there and so because our own kitchen was too tiny we all had to squeeze onto the upper outside porch, plates balanced precariously on our knees. It was then that everyone agreed that in future it might be better for them to stagger their holidays. It turned out to be a wise decision. I found I could enjoy the children and grandchildren more and give them more time if I could see them separately.

Needless to say, the day they all flew out, the sun returned and September and October were gloriously hot. Although the stables were full of workman returning after the August shut-down I managed to grab a daily swim in privacy as the pool was sheltered by the barn. The best time to swim of course was between noon and two when they all disappeared to the local café for their four- course lunch, with wine of course, and the cement mixer had stopped churning. Amazingly though, a four-course lunch never seemed to prevent them working and I was pleasantly surprised to find that the French workmen worked incredibly hard all day long. They never expected me to provide tea or coffee and often arrived at 8.00a.m worked unceasingly through until 12.00 then from 2.00 to 6.00. Not only that but they cleaned up each night, sweeping up the debris and taking it to the bins. A few cigarette ends were tossed in the flower beds but it was a small price to pay.

What bliss those lunchtime swims were. The silence was luxurious, the turquoise waters deliciously refreshing. Far above the deep blue sky was criss-crossed by tiny silver planes journeying to Africa, or northern Europe, leaving behind them trails of fluffy clouds.

Then one day something quite magical happened. Several swallows suddenly swept down alongside me, scooping up water in their beaks before soaring back into the sky. Back they came, again and again. I carried on swimming – enchanted - as they skimmed past my nose whirling around my head. It was if they had decided to come and play. What an unforgettable moment it had been. Who knows, maybe they were bringing me greetings from Africa?

As December drew closer we began to get anxious. There was still no tiling in the bathrooms nor a kitchen in the converted stables. Without the floors down the kitchen units couldn't be delivered, neither could the showers, bath and toilets be fitted in the bathrooms. At the same time I was having to liaise with the kitchen people who had already given us a date for fitting which we'd had to abort. They were now booked up for around Christmas and were threatening us with a new January slot. Getting everything to fit together it was like trying to get three up on a fruit machine.

Being angry clearly wouldn't work so I had to appeal to their better nature in my less than perfect French. Monsieur S the tiler was unmoved. He shrugged his shoulders as only a Frenchman seems able to do and stated he thought he couldn't come until January. 'But my family are arriving for Christmas, what will they do?' I pleaded. He shrugged again and disappeared to another job.

That afternoon I rushed down to his shop where his pretty wife ruled the roost. I told her the sad tale as best I could and hoped that she would be able to do something. At 8.00 the next morning Monsieur S arrived and the kitchen tiles were laid. I thanked him profusely, complimenting him on his work. 'Vous êtes, artiste, Monsieur S.' and then urged him to get the bathrooms finished. Meanwhile the bath, showers and toilets were stacked in the barn.

We then rushed off to Cahors to see the kitchen people and they agreed to give us a few hours before Christmas but on different days and unfortunately with different fitters. The delivery was finally made and we had to pay the remainder of the money on the spot before they would unload. This was not a good idea as we were then left without any leverage when we discovered there were many missing pieces, and half the units were in the wrong colour. So began days of arguments, lost tempers and frustrated tears. But eventually there was enough of a kitchen to make the Christmas cooking possible. It took another two months before everything was completed in the kitchen. I swore that my new kitchen would be bought elsewhere.

Suddenly the turmoil was over. The workmen left for their holidays and we unpacked Hannah's boxes, carried over her beds and furniture from the barn, hung up pictures and bought masses of house plants. The first thing she did that evening was to put on a CD, light some candles and invite us in for champagne. We looked around in amazement. It was hard to believe that six months ago this room had held two horse boxes, that the splendid kitchen was once a workshop, her bedroom a summer kitchen, and that the spacious beamed upstairs bedrooms and bathroom were once a cavernous old loft reached by a rickety ladder. We took a deep breath and raised our glasses. Apart from a few adjustments stage one was completed. Stage two was to begin on January 2nd.

But in the meantime we had a week of festivity with all the family. The weather was kind – the children played outside in t-shirts or light sweaters. We strolled through the woods in pale sunshine and had no idea then just how cold it was going to get. The unexpected frosts that froze the swimming pool and killed so many plants would not to arrive for another month and by then we would once again be in the midst of building chaos . But for the moment we just enjoyed the magic of being together and living an almost normal life.

In the evenings we visited the local town where the grandchildren were mesmerized by the Christmas lights and shrieked with delight as they rode the carousel. They ate slices of Pizzas from the local takeaway and drank hot chocolate before finally crashing into bed leaving the grown- ups to gorge themselves on oysters and Chablis, *foie gras* and chilled Sauternes. One of our favourite dinners was **duck breasts with honey and lemon***

So our first year in France was almost over. It had been exhausting and exciting – but we still had a long way to go before we could sit back and say 'Well, we've done it! The houses are finally finished, the workmen have gone and we're back to a normal family life'.

As I slipped into sleep my mind would be a jumble of images, past and present. France and Africa swirled around my head in a confusing kalaidescope of colours, smells and tastes, landscapes and faces. How vivid the memories of those first days in Eastern Nigeria – the shock, the squalor, the poverty. And yet what adventures I had enjoyed, and what adventures, I hoped, still lay ahead.

25

ENTENTE CORDIALE

One afternoon the following spring, as another great river the Lot flowed serenely past, Jacques turned up in time for coffee clutching a still warm clafoutis which he had just made – a different recipe from ours of the previous year, but still delicious. This trading of gifts we discovered was an important part of village life. Before our hens arrived Mme T. the village's oldest resident would insist on giving us eggs from her own hens. And on May Day she left a small bouquet of lilies of the valley in our porch. By this time she had insisted that we call her Memette, which in French means Little Gran, and is the name by which she was known by everyone in the village. It is apparently the tradition to make a gift of lilies of the valley on the first of May to those you consider your friends. She telephoned and in her strong local accent made sure that I brought them in and put them in water.

We were very touched and I hunted around our garden to see if I could find something of our own to offer. But all I could find were two beautiful deep pink roses which had just opened.. I took them to her and explained that the rose was the symbolic flower of England. She raised her thin and worn face to mine and bestowed a kiss on each cheek. Some weeks before I had taken her a small tart in thanks for the many eggs she given us before our own were laying – only to discover that she was diabetic. But still she was very gracious and no doubt gave it to one of her many daughters. She insisted that I sat down whilst she brought out photographs of her children, grandchildren and great grandchildren. Fortunately I wasn't required to say too much –' *si beau, si belle, si jolie'* - kept me going for the rest of the afternoon. I gathered from neighbours that she has wonderful natural remedies for colds, headaches, cuts and burns, using the plants in her garden. I was especially bemused by a cure for a headache which she gave me, which was to go to bed putting my feet on a bar of soap. Sometime later I tried it and when I woke up the headache had indeed gone – so who am I to doubt her?

In the autumn of that year, her daughter Monique left a bag of *cèpes,* those delicious and much sought-after mushrooms, on our gate. During the past few years this edible Boletus has been disappearing fast. Their whereabouts are carefully guarded secrets and although we had discovered many fungi in our own woods we were far too cautious to try eating them – especially since we'd heard that there was a 'false' *cèpe* which was definitely not to be tried. But then again we were told that the false *cèpe* is bright red, so we'd easily recognize it! Although it is possible in France to walk into your local pharmacy where they are trained to know the difference between edible and poisonous - (I have heard it said that is one reason the pharmacies are open on Sunday mornings because that's when families are out mushroom hunting) - I still felt happier just buying them from the old farmers' market stalls in the belief that if the farmers were still alive my chances were pretty good. Monique did not tell me where she picked them which was understandable but I know they do well where the sweet chestnuts grow and where there is plenty of summer sun and September rain. She waved her hand vaguely down the valley and the following autumn we saw her car parked on a small track leading into the woods.

Cèpes are very substantial and recognizable by their sponge-like gills. Never having bought fresh *cèpes* before I wasn't quite sure what to do with them. Monique gave me a suggestion for her **cèpes salad*** she was about to make and which turned out to be delicious.

* * *

Once we were in France we somehow felt the need to wave the British flag occasionally and put to rest the idea that the English couldn't cook. We decided to introduce our French neighbours to some typically English culinary delights – and perhaps the best way was a Sunday lunch.

Our first lunch was for Claude and Micheline, the couple from whom we had bought the house. They had moved to the hamlet thirty years ago from Paris when Claude set up his own accountancy business. But like us they had felt they needed one final project on retirement. Having decided that the Quercy farmhouse, outbuildings, pool and forty odd acres of woodland and meadows were too much, they sold to us. But they kept a few acres on the other side of the lane and had built a very modern and chic new house, known to us as 'the hacienda.'

We decided on steak and kidney pie, caramelized carrots, roast parsnips, green cabbage and pureèd potatoes. This was followed by a little cheese, including stilton which we could buy from an English- owned cheese stall in the market, and then hot lemon pudding with cream. The cheese before pudding is not a habit we've acquired in France, it's something we've always done in order to finish off the red wine and then have an excuse for opening a sweet dessert wine. But these days it's only when we're entertaining that we eat puddings – the rest of the time it's cheese or fresh fruit.

The roast parsnips however were a complete mystery to Claude and Micheline. I translated – '*panais*'. They were still confused. Perhaps I'd got the word or pronunciation wrong? Out came the dictionary. Amazingly they didn't even recognize the French word. I think the French probably use parsnips for cattle fodder if anything. Nevertheless they both seemed keen to try and even decided they liked them, accepting second helpings.

The second lunch was for Jacques and Nicole and this time we decided on roast beef and Yorkshire pudding. The butchers' shops in France are wonderful. Meat is lovingly prepared, often ready-tied for pot-roasting, sometimes rolled and beautifully stuffed with various delectable fillings. They make their own *terrines,* stuffed cabbage, *brandade de morue* (salt cod, mashed potato and garlic), couscous salad, pigs' trotters and sausages made of unmentionable parts. Outside there is usually a large blackboard which tells you the breed of animal, and the name and address of the farmer. The butcher I use is Pascal, the husband of Memette's granddaughter – it's amazing how many of the local businesses are run by her family members – who are delightfully helpful. It's a good job as one of my big problems to start with was learning about the different cuts of meat. It took me some months before I sorted out the best cuts for braising for example. I now often use *jarret*, which is the equivalent to our shin beef.

Because I was anxious that we had enough meat for the lunch party, I ordered two ribs from the butcher, carefully emphasizing that I wanted the two ribs together and not cut into two separate ones. The previous Christmas I had ordered a three- rib piece and when I collected it found three separate ribs. But the bigger shock had been the price, they had cost me the equivalent of sixty pounds! This time I was prepared for the price, but not for the size which was enormous. And so again was the price. I tried to persuade myself that forty-five pounds spread over several days meals wasn't too bad especially in such a good cause.   Not sure I succeeded, and by the end of the week we were fed up with trying to find something interesting to do with rare cold beef.

As the lunch for Jacques and Nicole was near Christmas, I decided that I should make them the traditional **Christmas trifle*** which has been a family favourite handed down from my mother-in-law, Edith. It was a great success.

My only problem came when I tried to translate the word 'trifle'. Searching through the dictionary I decided that the word '*bagatelle*' would do very well. It meant 'a small thing' which is how I would translate a ' mere trifle'. But of course the French language is full of pitfalls.

I wondered why Jacques burst out laughing when I offered him a ' bagatelle.' 'Avec plaisir' he grinned. Then he explained that in France ' une bagatelle' refers to a pre-adulterous flirtation! Edith would not have been amused

*   *   *

A few months later, Jacques and Nicole invited us for dinner. He'd asked me once what food we particularly enjoyed and I had aid we loved *cassoulet* which is perhaps the most famous of SW France's dishes. Basically it is white haricot beans, sausage, smoked ham and *confit* of duck or goose. So when we received our invitation I wondered if that is what would be on the menu, and if so who else would be invited, as *cassoulets* are usually prepared for at least eight people.

No-one ever turns up for a dinner or lunch in France without bearing suitable gifts. We had discovered that both our French neighbours were extremely generous. Claude and Micheline had arrived with chilled champagne and a bouquet of flowers. Jacques and Nicole came bearing a hugely expensive pineapple plant complete with pineapple and a bottle of very expensive wine. We always find it a bit risky taking Cahors wines to our knowledgeable neighbours, so usually buy something special from another region. You rarely find wines from the New World in French wine shops, except maybe in Paris and the larger cities.

That afternoon I went to the nursery and bought for Jacques and Nicole a large white orchid plant, bursting with exotic blooms. We discovered early on that the magnificent potted chrysanthemums you see are strictly for the dead. On All Saints' Day, November 1st everyone goes back to their village and takes a potted chrysanthemum to their relatives' graves.

It was dark as we set off across the lane. But to our surprise and delight, Nicole had lit dozens of small candles and had lined the route from our door to theirs, across the lane and garden and up their stone steps. She had done the same from Monique and Jacques' house, so we knew that they would be there too. The other guests were already standing around the huge log fire sipping aperitifs. The last two guests were Nicole's mother Simone, and her husband René who lived further down the lane.

No-one spoke a word of English of course (although Nicole understands more than she admits to) so we knew this was going to be quite a challenging night. One to one in French isn't too bad, but when six French people talk to each other....! The speed is so rapid and of course the local accent and slang expressions are incredibly confusing. Ideally of course you need a clear head to cope, but I decided that a few drinks would take away the tension and I might even understand more. Well, if not, at least I wouldn't mind too much. But surprisingly we managed to join in and once we got them to slow down and repeat the jokes in idiot- proof language we had a really good time.

The appetizers were hot *foie gras* wrapped in small filo pastry parcels, and *foie gras quenelles* – small dumplings made of pounded *foie gras*, bound with egg and poached in salted water. They were offered with a glass of sweet white wine, well to be exact several glasses. By the time we sat down to eat I was already feeling pretty bloated and light-headed.

Jacques put down on the table a large *terrine* pot, complete with a hen-shaped lid. Inside was his own home-made rabbit and mushroom *paté*. Served with small gherkins and bread it was delicious and incredibly filling. I wondered how I was going to manage the *cassoulet*. The huge dish was placed lovingly in the centre of the table bubbling and steaming beneath a golden breadcrumb crust.

There are three main kinds of *cassoulets;* those of Castelnaudary, of Carcassonne, and of Toulouse. All are based on white haricot beans and are prepared with various combinations of pork, mutton, preserved goose or duck, and sausage. The Toulouse *cassoulet* Jacques had prepared included belly pork, preserved duck and sausage.

Anatole France loved the *cassoulet* and in **Histoire Comique** he wrote:

'I am going to lead you to a little tavern in the rue Vavin, *chez Clémence*, who only makes one dish, but a stupendous one; *le cassoulet de Castlenaudary* which contains legs of *confit d'oie* (preserved goose), haricot beans previously blanched, pork fat, and little sausages. To be good it must have cooked very slowly for a long time. *Clémence's cassoulet* has been cooking for twenty years. She replenishes the pot sometimes with goose, sometimes with pork fat, sometimes she puts in a sausage or some haricots, but it is always the same *cassoulet*. The basis remains, and this ancient and precious substance gives it a savour, which one finds in the paintings of the old Venetian master, in the amber flesh tints of their women. Come, I wish you to taste *Clémence's cassoulet*'.

That evening Jacques raided his wonderful wine cellar. I hate to think how many bottles we drank but he insisted that we try various years to compare the taste. I remember claiming that I preferred a '96 to a '97 but I'm not sure my palate could really tell the difference after the number of glasses I'd downed. And I can't even remember now which wine it was. But the overall effect was delightful and I could have sworn my French improved enormously.

Of course no French meal is complete without the cheese course and we were presented with a large selection of soft and hard cheeses, new and old goats' cheese, and especially for us Stilton. None of the other French guests had tasted Stilton and there was a look of trepidation on their faces as Jacques insisted they try a little. You would have thought they were being offered poison. Shakes of heads all around. René grimaced and shuddered. 'Orrible,' he declared, claiming it was too dry.

By now I could scarcely move and was in need of a long lie down in a darkened room. But that wasn't going to be easy. The door opened and in marched Simone, Nicole's mother with a gigantic Baked Alaska – *Omelette Norwegienne*. If only we could have had a three hour break I would have enjoyed it much more but even so it was delectable There was no way after that, that I could swallow another thing. But Jacques brought out at least six different bottles of *digestifs*, among them Armagnac, Cognac, and his own *Eau de Vie*. All I could manage was a small cup of very strong coffee.

David and I were the first to leave in the early hours of the morning, thinking how lucky we were to have discovered in our new life such wonderful and friendly neighbours.

The candles had burnt out but above us the stars shone brilliantly in the black frosty air. Somewhere in Africa maybe someone too was gazing upwards like me, only for them the night would be warm, the breeze gentle. For a moment I thought longingly of the huge skies of the Dark Continent and of those two great rivers, the Niger and the Nile which had meandered so wonderfully through my life.

But they belonged to our past, and it was now time to relish that other great river, the Lot, which now flowed serenely through the valley below.

26

WINING AND DINING

I cannot deny that shopping, cooking, eating and drinking, (moderately of course) are some of our lives' greatest pleasures.

When David asks first thing in the morning, 'What are the plans today?' he really means 'Where are we shopping, what are we buying and who's doing the cooking?' Sometimes it's code for 'Shall we go out for lunch today?'

When we first met, David was certainly the more experienced cook. He'd travelled widely and learnt to appreciate different foods, was more innovative and daring than I was. But my love of cooking developed over the years and was a creative outlet for me especially when I was at home with our children. We would often spend our weekends with them making our own pasta, rolling it out and hanging it over the ceiling clothes' rack to dry. There's a lot to be said for large Victorian kitchens.

As a consequence our three children are passionate and expert cooks and these days recipes fly back and forth between them via the email. If one of us goes out to eat everyone else wants to know exactly what it was we ate and how it was cooked. Our two daughters-in-law were somewhat bemused when they first joined the family. 'Why is it', asked Francesca 'that within five minutes of getting together one of you is discussing a new recipe you've tried, talking about a new product you've seen in the supermarket, or planning the next family meal?' But I've noticed that both she and Lisa are becoming serious gourmets themselves. I suppose it's a case of 'if you can't beat them….!'

Our local market is held on Fridays. It runs in a huge circle around the church, overflowing into the narrow side streets. Each stall is protected by a colourful striped canopy, shading the owners from the burning sun, or in the winter, the bitter winds. The first time we visited I just walked round and round, overwhelmed by such choice, such fine quality. In England the markets are places to find the good bargains, the cheaper products. But it is very different in France. Only the very best goods are for sale, and often much more expensive than in the supermarket. What I love above all are the little old ladies, dressed in the ubiquitous housecoat, ankle socks and slippers, selling a small basket of walnuts, a bunch of dahlias, a dozen newly laid eggs. In fact anything they have spare from their kitchen garden which will make a few centimes.

On my first visit, drawn to the fish stall I found some delicious crevettes. I looked at the price and decided on a kilo as we had a large lunch party that day. Madame looked patiently at this obvious 'foreigner'. 'Madame' she sighed 'that is the price for one hundred grams.' After that I bought all my crevettes from the supermarket where, although previously frozen from Brazil or Madagascar, a kilo could be bought for the same price as the one hundred grams from the fish stall. There really was not much difference in the taste especially if served with **homemade mayonnaise*** or curried sauce.

As the months went by I became more confident and discerning and learnt which was the best cheese stall – although occasionally I would be unfaithful when a new one arrived. I suppose the most common cheese that is found locally and served in every restaurant is a tiny round cheese - the size of a coffee saucer - made from raw goats milk. In Langue d'Oc, the old language of the south, it is known as cabécou. It matures quickly and has a thin rind of natural mould and a tender creamy flesh (pate). **Goat's Cheese salad*** is a family favourite.*

However I rarely buy fruit and vegetables from the market – except maybe for the new season's prunes, melons or small woodland strawberries. Not that all the products aren't wonderful, but we have a first- class greengrocers in the town, who has branched out into a small cheese, olive and dried- fruit delicatessen. The shop is air-conditioned so that even on a blazing summer's day, the vegetables are fresh and firm. The staff are friendly and clearly passionate about the food they sell. Even though they are more expensive than the market stalls I'd hate to see them close down so feel I must support them.

When I go in and ask for melons for example, the first question is 'when for?' If I say, one for today, one for tomorrow and one for Sunday, they will lovingly test each one in the shop, then go to the storeroom behind and finally emerge with three melons each one numbered carefully so that I eat the right one on the right day. I can't imagine many greengrocers in England doing that for me.

But what is even more delightful is seeing the seasons reflected in the shops. I see very little that is flown in from afar, tasting of nothing in particular. Instead we live on what grows naturally during its rightful season. It's possible to walk into the shop and immediately know what month it is.

Hannah's **Orange Marmalade*** is great favourite with family, friends and neighbours, and everyone eagerly awaits the arrival in January of the Seville oranges. At the same time her kitchen is filled with the heady smells of **Vin d'Oranges*** so delicious drunk ice- cold as an aperitif or as a digestif after a rich meal.

As the weather warms up and the swallows swoop across the sky we eat outside as much as possible. There's nothing more wonderful than spending a summer evening by the pool with friends and family, the table filled with candles and the pool floodlit. One of our special meals for such a night would be a starter of fresh crevettes served with homemade mayonnaise and followed by a **game terrine*** and green salad followed by **peaches and redcurrants in Riesling***

*   *   *

The department of the Lot is renowned for its wine, its walnuts and its truffles. Since the times of the Greeks and Romans the black truffle has been treasured as an aphrodisiac, a medicine and a culinary delicacy whose reputation, I have to admit, I find hard to appreciate.

Known as 'the black diamond' this dark brown fungus grows on chalky barren soils, and is found on the roots of certain trees, especially the oak. It is round, normally varying in size from a large walnut to a very large plum. But there have been records of some as large as a man's fist. Above all it has a very pungent odour which flavours everything in its vicinity.

It is found mainly in those areas of South West France such as Perigord and Quercy where the land is capable of supporting only scrubby trees, juniper and a few wild flowers and grasses. But even in perfect conditions the truffle doesn't always survive and over the years it has been in decline. This is partly due to the exodus of the farming population following the devastating effect of phylloxera, a disease which wiped out the vines at the end of the 19th century. People left for the towns to find work and were no longer around to harvest the truffle - their other source of income. Then came the 1914-18 war when so many young men lost their lives and the countryside became unmanned, unloved and unproductive.

But its disappearance is also due to changes in the climate and the environment. The problem is that the truffle guards its secrets and taunts its would-be harvesters so that no-one seems to be quite sure how to improve its production. These days specially trained dogs seem to have replaced the pig when it comes to sniffing out the powerful aroma of the truffle which is detectable, they say, even when it's half-a-metre underground. So a good hunting dog is worth its weight in gold and is highly prized and carefully guarded from would-be abductors.

Today there are all kinds of experiments to re-introduce the truffle – the planting of new oaks as well as the development of different strains of oaks. Land is being cleared and hopeful farmers are trying different techniques of fertilization in hope of once again cornering the market. For the truffle lives up to its name of 'black diamond' as it fetches extremely high prices as chefs from all over the country descend on the area between November and March to attend the local truffle markets.

Not far away from us the famous truffle market is held each year in Lalbenque, a market town, south of Cahors . It is held at 2.00 p.m every Tuesday, normally between November and March. Needless to say Jacques was more than happy to go with us and said he would ring and reserve lunch for us at the local hotel. There we would be able to sample a truffle omelette as our main course. I could hardly wait.

I had read so much about the market, of the top Paris chefs flying down for the day; of furtive exchanges of paper bags, baskets and fistfuls of money. I had seen photographs of wonderfully wizened old faces – deeply lined and burnt nearly as brown as the truffle itself – and I was eager to photograph them for my own archives.

Normally the main thoroughfare is lined on either side with trestle-tables, but that year we had suffered a devastating heatwave which had not only affected the vines, but also the truffles. The yield was very poor and consequently the price very high. There were perhaps only a dozen tables on one side of the road. There was no sign of buyers or sellers, but then we had to wait for the bell to ring at 2.00 p.m. before the action began.

The restaurant was crowded. I looked around wondering if it were possible to spot any top chefs. It wasn't. But maybe they knew something about the quality of the cooking and had made other arrangements. It was an expensive meal by local standards and very indifferent. The much longed- for truffle omelette was very disappointing. I should think they'd used tinned truffles, or so little of the real thing that there was no flavour at all.

As 2.00 p.m. approached I went outside with my camera. By now the streets had started to fill up. A crowd of very smartly dressed businessmen hovered around puffing on cigars and greeting all and sundry profusely. Local council elections were shortly to take place and politicians, being what they are, never miss an opportunity to press the flesh. The sellers had arrived with their baskets and bags and scales. There were some wonderful faces to capture on film but difficult to do so without their knowing. I caught sight of a local well-known chef who runs a Michelin- starred restaurant in the village next to ours. Jacques had told me that I would be able to smell the truffles as soon as I got outside. But I didn't. Maybe the scorching summer and long drought had taken its toll or maybe all the cigar smoke just masked it.

There was an official set of scales provided by the town where weights could be checked. But it was hard to see much money changing hands, although clearly it was. Years of practice had turned them into magicians, experts in sleight-of- hand Looking around I wondered if any tax men were there with their cameras?

It was all over in fifteen minutes. Apparently this was to be the last market as the season had been so poor it wasn't worth continuing for another month. Maybe I'll go back one year when the weather has been good and the crop heavy. I might even get to like the taste, but in the meantime I'll continue to have my omelettes with *cèpes*.

27

HOME AT LAST

I t's now seven years since the furniture van trundled up the hill to our farmhouse in France and I think I can finally say that it feels like home.

But there have been times when I've felt a stranger in a strange land. I've found my lack of fluency in the language a real frustration. Being able to read the newspaper or novels in French, which I can and do, is very different from holding an intelligent conversation. Not being able to express myself fluently sometimes makes me feel as if I've lost my personality.

How can a Frenchman know what I'm really like when I mumble and stutter and grope for words? How can I express wit, or humour, anger or disdain, all the things that I'm good at doing in my own language? Being able to express myself clearly and succinctly has been so important throughout my life and career. Writing, giving talks, chairing courts, selling ideas and running conferences is what I did best. It gave shape to who I was. Now that I can no longer do them it's as if I've lost part of myself.

I think it's a problem that many ex-pats don't foresee when they fall in love with the idea of a new life in a new country. They forget that they are leaving behind not only their family and friends but also their comforting routines, their knowledge of how the system works, their sense of belonging.

Spending a two- week holiday in the sun, drinking wine around the pool and eating cheaply in local bistros maybe seductive, but it's not real life. The reality is that it rains, the winters are cold, the shops close at noon for two hours and the bureaucracy drives you mad. You can stamp your feet but can't say what you want to say. The rapid replies and explanations are completely unintelligible, and when you ask them to slow down, they say it all over again at exactly the same pace. I've met many people whose dreams became nightmares and who are now struggling to sell up and go back home.

I suppose that having been used to being an ex-patriot, (I'd also spent a year living and working in Israel before I met David), it has been easier for us to live in a country that is not our own. It really doesn't seem so very different from our past life. We've met many people here who have also spent some of their working lives overseas and it's noticeable that they, and the ones who have family here, are the ones who settle more easily.

But, and it's a big but, there are wonderful compensations to living in France. The French are warm and friendly and very helpful. The pace of life is slow and relaxed and no-one complains when shop assistants engage in long conversations with a customer whilst the queue grows, or drivers stop in the middle of the road to enquire about the state of the vines with the local farmer.

We can get in the car and within a few hours can be sitting by the Atlantic or Mediterranean sipping chilled wine. We can picnic on glorious patès and ripe peaches in the foothills of the Pyrenees or in the valleys of the Lot and Dordogne. In the winter we can wander though the colourful Christmas market in Bordeaux, buy 'santon', the nativity figures from Provence and drink hot chocolate in steamy cafés. We can take the train after breakfast and be in Paris for lunch and England for dinner. What more could we ask?

My days are now filled with writing, painting, reading, learning Tai Chi and of course cooking. I have a group of friends with whom I enjoy coffee, lunch or dinner. Together we've raised a great deal of money for cancer charities by holding a book sale each Christmas.

Hannah finally met and married a charming Frenchman, Sébastian, and they now have two delightful daughters, Inès and Céleste. Both Sébastian, who studied in China, and his mother Mauricette have introduced us to more delicious recipes. His **Hong Shao Rou*** is a flavoursome pork dish which is now a family favourite, whilst Mauricette's **Pea, Potato and Carrot Casserole*** is simple, easy and very comforting.

We are so lucky to have six beautiful grandchildren in England and France. We see Alice and Jessica and Theo and Isabel as often as we can and they all bring us so much happiness and contentment. This book was written mainly for them, so that one day they may appreciate that Granny was not always an old lady, but once led a youthful, fascinating and exciting life.

As I sit on my wooden terrace, lovingly built by David, and look down to the woods and the lake I could so easily be back in Africa. But instead of the elephant at the watering hole we have the deer. Instead of the roar of the lion we have the barking of the fox, and instead of the cry of the fish-eagle we have the screech of the green woodpecker. It will do.

Now each spring I content myself with awaiting the return of the swallows who bring with them memories of my beloved Africa. In the summers we swim together once again beneath the cloudless skies. And when they depart in the autumn, a little of my heart goes with them.

* * *

RECIPES

SAVOURY DELIGHTS

Kofta
Curried meatballs

For 6

500g mince beef or beef/pork

3 cloves of garlic paste (make by grating cloves finely)

3 tsp ginger paste

2 tsp garam masala

2 tbsp fresh coriander

A handful of fresh breadcrumbs, soaked and squeezed

Salt and pepper

Mix together and form into large walnut sized balls. If the mixture seems too dry add a beaten egg. Set aside

Curry Sauce

2 tbsp groundnut oil

3 large onions finely sliced

1 tsp mustard seeds

4 cardamom seeds

1 sliver of cinnamon stick

small tin of tomatoes

2 tsp tomato puree

2 tbsp each of ginger and garlic paste

2 tsp chilli powder

1 tsp turmeric powder

2 tbsp coriander powder

1 tsp cumin powder

salt

water

Heat the oil and when hot cook the mustard seeds until sizzling. Then add the cardamom seeds, cinnamon and finally onion. Reduce heat and cook until onions begin to brown. Add all the other ingredients, cook for a couple of minutes, finally adding enough water to cover the meatballs which are placed gently in the sauce. Simmer for about 20/25 mins, taking care not to break the meatballs when stirring the curry.

Before serving sprinkle with 1 tsp garam masala, and a handful of fresh coriander leaves. Serve with rice and/or naan bread.

Groundnut Stew (Peanut Stew)

For 4

4 large chicken pieces

2 tbsp oil

1 onion finely chopped

250g okra (substitute green beans if necessary)

1 ½ tsp salt

½ tsp pepper

2 tbsp tomato paste

small tin crushed tomatoes

¼ tsp cayenne

450ml water

250g peanut butter

Heat the oil in a large pot. Season the chicken pieces and cook until browned, about ten minutes. Remove from pan. Leaving small amount of oil in the pan soften the onion, stir in the tomato paste and the tomatoes together with the cayenne. Return the chicken to the pot and stir in 350 ml of the water. Simmer for about ten minutes.

Mix the remaining water with the peanut butter until smooth and add to the pot. Simmer until the chicken is almost cooked and then add the okra for the last ten minutes.

Serve with rice.

Magret de Canard au Miel et au Citron
(Duck breast with honey and lemon)

For 4

2 duck breasts

3 lemons

2 tbsp honey

2 tbsp oil

Sauce –

    2 tbsp butter

    2 tbsp flour

    200 ml chicken stock

    salt & pepper

chervil

Peel two of the lemons and quarter. Carefully peel the third lemon, and cut the peel into fine strips. Blanche in boiling water for a minute. Squeeze the juice of the third lemon. Reserve. Heat the oil in a frying pan and cook the magrets, fat side down first. Turn after five minutes (or until skin has browned and the fat reduced) and continue to cook until ready. Remove and keep warm. Drain any fat from the pan and add the honey, pour in the lemon juice and bring to the boil.

Make the sauce by melting the butter in a saucepan, add the flour and cook until brown, then add chicken stock and stir until thicken.

Place sliced magret onto each plate with a lemon quarter, pour over sauce. Decorate with lemon peel and sprinkle with chervil.

Rabbit and Chicken Terrine

Streaky bacon - enough to line a terrine dish
1 Rabbit
Chicken livers 250 g (foie gras is better!)
2 chicken breasts thinly sliced
Belly pork (same weight as rabbit meat)
Vermouth/brandy
2 onions
4 cloves of garlic
pistachio nuts (according to your taste)
1 tbsp green peppercorns
bay leaves
thyme
pepper and sea salt
goose/duck fat

Gently fry the onions in the fat until soft and translucent, put on one side. Remove the meat from the rabbit. Finely chop all the meat by hand but not the chicken breasts. Mix in the onions, the crushed garlic, plenty of salt and pepper. Add pistachios and/or green peppercorns and whatever alcohol you're using to make a moist mixture.

Stretch the bacon with the back of the knife and line your terrine dish having laid a couple of bay leaves on the bottom on the dish. (When it's turned out the bottom becomes the top and will look decorative.) Leave enough bacon hanging over the edges so that it can be folded over when the terrine is full. Half fill with mixture, then slice the chicken breasts thinly lengthways and cover w the mixture. Lay the remaining mixture on top. Then place a couple of rashers of bacon along the top and fold over the bacon so that the terrine is enclosed. Place another bay leaf on top and cover with tinfoil.

Leave to rest for a couple of hours with some heavy weights to compact the terrine.

Remove weights and cook at 150 deg C in a *bain marie* with the water half way up the side of the terrine for about 2 hrs. Test with skewer and make sure the juices are clear and the centre hot.

Once cooled, refrigerate. Can keep for up to 2 weeks. Serve thinly sliced with gerkins and/or onion marmalade, green salad and fresh baguettes. Don't forget the wine

Sebastien's Hong Shao Rou Spicy Pork

for 4

600-900g of fresh belly pork

2 large cloves of garlic

4-6 star anise

1 stick of cinnamon

3 tbsp finely chopped fresh ginger

3 tbsp sugar

6 tbsp dark mushroom soy sauce

1 glass of sherry

oil

Cut the pork into half inch cubes and bring to the boil in a saucepan of water. Drain and boil for a second time. Drain and run under cold water.

In the meantime, slice the ginger and garlic into small matchsticks. Put a tbsp of oil in a wok and put in the ginger. Cook until golden, then add garlic but don't let it burn. Now add the pork and cook over fierce heat. Let the meat brown a little then add the sherry. Using a wooden spoon, scrape the bottom of the wok, loosening any sticking food. Add the soy sauce and then the star anise, the cinnamon and sugar. Pour in two glasses of water (enough to cover the meat). Cover the wok and simmer slowly for a minimum of 2 hours. Uncover for the last 20 minutes to reduce the sauce.

It should be thick enough to coat the back of a wooden spoon. Serve with rice and stir-fry vegetables.

Fricandelles
(Meatballs in Tomato sauce)

For 6

400g sausage meat

400g minced beef

2 eggs

200g soft bread soaked in milk

Bunch chives

Bunch parsley

100g flour

3 tbsp goose fat (or cooking oil)

3 onions

3 glasses of light beer

1 tbsp tomato concentrate

bouquet garni

salt and pepper

Mix together the sausage meat, beef and bread (squeezed dry), eggs, chives, parsley, salt and pepper. Then make into small balls, roll in flour and fry in the oil. When they are golden, remove. Then chop the onions and fry in the same pan as before, add the tomato concentrate, beer salt and pepper. Add the meat balls and cook gently for about 40 mins.

West African Chicken Kebabs

6 chicken breasts

(750g pork or lamb work just as well)

4 onions, chopped

2 tsp grated ginger

2 tsp grated garlic

30g plain flour

60g unsalted, dry roasted peanuts, ground.

2 large ripe tomatoes (tinned will do)

1 tbsp Tabasco sauce

red and green peppers optional

Mix the ingredients into a large bowl, with the chicken or meat into cut into cubes and allow to marinate overnight, or at least one hour if you're short of time. If using peppers, cut into small pieces and marinate also.

Remove the meat and peppers and place on skewers. Grill or barbeque until ready.

Sprinkle with another 30 gm of ground peanuts. You can always liquidize the remaining marinade and serve with meat another day.

Jolliffe Rice

This is a one pot dish eaten all over West Africa. There's no set recipe you simply use what you have. Basically you fry onions and garlic in ground-nut oil together with chopped tomatoes and red peppers. You can add any other spices such as ginger and chilli, nutmeg and cumin. Add the rice and cover with chicken or vegetable stock and cook until the rice has taken up all the stock and is cooked. Add chopped cooked meat, chicken and vegetables such as okra

Avocadoes with Prawns and Homemade Mayonnaise

Crayfish are wonderful if you can get them. But it's easier of course to buy ready cooked prawns. Simply shell them, then make your mayonnaise by taking one egg yolk, squeeze of lemon juice, salt and pepper, then slowly drizzle in 1/4pt oil beating continuously until thickened. I then add a tsp of hot water which lightens the mayonnaise. Add more lemon juice and seasoning. I often add some tomato puree (tomato ketchup will do just as well), a dash of Worcestershire sauce and a pinch of paprika and this makes an excellent prawn cocktail sauce. Sometimes I peel the avocado and slice onto the plate, otherwise I halve, remove the stone and fill with prawns coated with sauce.

Prawns or Shrimps in Marinade

1 onion cut into fine rings

4 bay leaves

230 ml of oil (groundnut or sunflower)

110 ml of white vinegar

3 tbsp capers (with liquid)

2 tsp celery seeds

1 ½ tsp salt

few drops of Tabasco

Mix together the shrimps, the thinly slices onion and bay leaves. Pour over the marinade and leave 12 -24 hrs. Drain. Delicious if placed in centre of tomato ring mousse!

Roasted Vegetables – serve hot or cold

Onions

Aubergines

Courgettes

Tomatoes

Peppers

Garlic

Olive oil

Salt and pepper

Gather a selection of various coloured vegetables, chop into large cubes and place in bowl. Sprinkle on plenty of olive oil, salt, pepper and using your hands mix thoroughly. In the meantime place a shallow baking tray, oiled, in hot oven 200degC, when it's hot tip on the vegetables and cook for about 45 mins or until the edges begin to turn black. These days I use whole cherry tomatoes and sometimes black olives.

Mauricette's Pea, Potato and Carrot Casserole

This is a great standby – almost a meal in itself. Simply adjust the quantities to suit yourself, your tastes and your visitors.

Fry some diced lardons in oil until cooked. Then add some chopped carrots and cubed potatoes and stir well. Sprinkle with large tbsp of flour and stir for a few minutes. Then pour over hot chicken stock. Add small packet of frozen peas, salt and pepper. Top up with more stock so that all the vegetables are just covered. Cover and cook slowly for at least 45 mins until the vegetables are cooked and the sauce thickened

Cheese and Onion Tart

Pastry Case
250g plain flour
pinch salt
125g fat (half butter and half lard)
cold water from fridge

Rub together the ingredients until like fine breadcrumbs, add enough water to make a firm dough. Leave in fridge for half an hour. Line a tart tin (metal) with the pastry, leaving any overlapping pastry. Place in fridge for ten minutes

Filling
Five medium onions
4 eggs
60g butter
4 tsp flour
300ml cream
125g grated cheese (I prefer strong)
salt and pepper

Peel and slice the onions finely and boil for 15 min. Strain and then sauté gently in the butter until golden brown. Beat the eggs and add the cream and the flour until smooth. Add the cheese, pepper and salt if needed. Fill the pastry case, roll off the extra pastry and place the case on a hot tray in the oven (this ensures the bottom will cook thoroughly). Cook until set - About 30 min. (If a visitor passed through and brought me some blue cheese from Lagos, I'd leave out the onions and sprinkle the blue cheese on top before cooking).

Cèpes and Potato Salad

Wipe the cèpes with damp kitchen paper and remove any earthy parts from the stalks. Fry small pieces of bacon (lardons) in oil. Meanwhile boil small waxy potatoes and then cube when cooked. Sauté the mushrooms, adding a little more oil if necessary. Season, mix all together. Add vinaigrette whilst warm. Then I threw in a few handfuls of rocket or watercress. Serve with French bread, chilled white or chilled light red.

Fig and Ham Salad

Jambon cru (dried country ham)
Goats' cheese/Mozzarella
Rocket and/or watercress
Vinaigrette (I think walnut oil is best for this)
Parmesan shavings

Simply quarter the figs, shred the dried ham by hand, crumble the cheese and toss everything together with the dressing. Serve with French bread and plenty of dry, cold wine.

Best eaten on the terrace by the pool under an azure blue sky.

Goat's Cheese Salad

These small round cheeses make wonderful starters, grilled and served on a small piece of toasted baguette, drizzled with honey and placed on a bed of salad. The salad should be lightly dressed with walnut oil vinaigrette and scattered with walnut pieces.

Tomato and Red Onion Salad

Slice tomatoes and onion. Layer in dish, sprinkling with olive oil, lemon juice and coarse salt. Add basil if you wish or even mozzarella cheese but….perhaps keep it simple!

Breaded Chicken Breast Ribbons

I prefer to slice chicken breasts in fine strips, rather in nuggets. Roll in seasoned flour, dip in beaten egg, then roll in breadcrumbs and fry in hot oil. You can add cayenne, or curry powder to the seasoned flour for a stronger taste. Drain on kitchen paper.

Asparagus With Country Ham

Snap off the woody part of the asparagus and peel if the stems are thick. Then take four pieces and wrap a slice of country ham around the middle . Place each bundle on a baking tray, drizzle with oil and bake in hot oven until cooked. About 15 mins.

Asparagus With Eggs and Butter

Clean and prepare the asparagus then cook in boiling water or steam, until tender. Meanwhile boil one egg per person until hard. Peel and grate into small individual dishes. Melt butter and pour into separate dishes. To eat, mix the butter and egg together and dip the asparagus into the mixture. Can be seasoned with nutmeg.

Homemade Crisps

Slice waxy potatoes as finely as possible. Drop into hot fat until cooked, removed onto kitchen paper and salt well. Parsnips are equally delicious.

Hollandaise Sauce with Curry

Yolks of 2 eggs

1 tsp water

100g warm clarified butter

1 tsp curry power

½ tsp paprika

squeeze of lemon

salt and pepper

Place bowl over saucepan of hot water and add the water, egg yolks salt and pepper.

Beat with a fork until the mixture whitens. Little by little add the butter continuing to beat until the mixture thickens. Add the lemon, curry and paprika. Serve warm on the fish.

Beer Batter for Fish

225g   self-raising flour

300ml light beer

salt

Sift the flour and salt, add the beer beating until smooth. Should be consistency of thick cream. Add more beer if necessary. Wipe the fish with kitchen paper and then dip in flour, this helps the batter stick. Make sure the oil is really hot before dropping in the fish

Lime and Coriander Dressing

1 tsp chilli paste
1 clove of garlic
2 spring onions
5cm piece fresh ginger
2 tbsp chopped fresh coriander
zest and juice of 2 limes
2 tsp sugar
2 tbsp groundnut oil
1 tbsp sesame oil
salt & pepper

Place garlic, ginger, coriander and onions in a food processor and roughly chop. Empty into mixing bowl and add remaining ingredients. Whisk until thoroughly mixed.

SWEET MEMORIES

Clafoutis

For 6

Heat oven to 180 C / 350 F / Mark 4

50g unsalted butter

2 eggs

2 egg yolks

60g plain flour

60g vanilla sugar

pinch salt

280 ml milk

500g stoned cherries

 Beat all the ingredients together, pour some into a heated and buttered pie dish, add cherries and pour rest of batter on top. Place back in oven and reduce temperature to about 170C and bake until golden brown. About 45 – 60min

Simple Fruit Cake

250g self raising flour

12 g butter

125g brown sugar

125g mixed fruit

1 large egg

2 tbsp warm milk

Sieve flour with a pinch of salt, add the fruit. In another bowl beat the butter and sugar until light then add the egg and milk. Stir in the fruit and flour mixture, turn into greased tin and bake for about an hour at 180C.

Chocolate Cake

120g butter

200g sugar

4 tbsp rich cocoa powder

6 tbsp hot water

120g flour

1 tsp baking powder

2 large eggs, separated

Mix butter, hot water and cocoa in a saucepan. Add sugar and beat well. Stir in sieved flour then the yolks of the eggs. Fold in the stiffly beaten whites carefully and bake for 40-45 minutes at 180C. You can of course top with melted chocolate – but not recommended for picnics in hot climates!

Chocolate Mousse

For 6
120g dark chocolate
30g butter
1 tbsp strong coffee
30ml Armagnac/Cognac
4 large eggs

Melt the chocolate, butter, brandy and coffee in bowl over hot water. Whisk until smooth. Leave to cool. Then add yolks to the mixture. Beat the whites until stiff and gently fold in. If you wish, crumble some Amaretto biscuits in the bottom of each ramekin.

Baked Figs

24 ripe figs
100g caster sugar
100g butter

Butter an oven-proof dish. Make two cuts on the top of each fig (quartering but not cutting all the way through). Place small nut of butter in each. Place in dish and sprinkle liberally with sugar. Bake in oven for about 15 mins at 180C. Serve warm with cream or ice-cream

Peaches and Redcurrants in Riesling

500g ripe peaches
500g redcurrants
100g sugar
1/2 litre of Riesling (I usually add the whole bottle as we love the juice!)

Peel the peaches, remove the stones and then quarter. Wash the redcurrants.

Put them all into pan with sugar and wine and cook gently for about 25 – 30 mins.

Cool, place in fridge and serve very cold

Bananas Cooked in Rum and Orange Juice

4 bananas
50g butter
2 tbsp brown sugar
6 tbsp rum/orange juice

Melt the butter in a frying pan, add the sugar and when sizzling add the rum and orange juice. Slice the banana lengthways and put into pan. Cook until soft and caramelized.

Clara's Crunchy Cookies

200g butter
140g soft brown sugar
240g plain flour
¼ tsp salt
1 large tbsp demerara sugar

Cream the butter and soft sugar until light. Add the flour and salt, mix to a firm dough.

Shape into biscuit sized cylinder and roll in the demerara sugar. Wrap in tinfoil and place in fridge for an hour. Slice into rounds and bake at 150C until golden.

Louise's Brownies

170g dark chocolate (at least 70%)
170g butter
300g sugar
125g flour
3 eggs
100g chopped mixed nuts (pecan, macadamia, brazils, hazelnuts)
vanilla
salt

Place the butter and chocolate in a bowl over hot water. Stir until melted, then add the sugar. Beat in the eggs and a few drops of vanilla. Mix thoroughly then add the sifted flour and salt. Add nuts.

Grease and flour a small baking tray - (the smaller the tray the thicker the brownies). Bake for about 35 min at 150C. Allow to cool in tin before cutting into squares.

Edith's Christmas Trifle

Sponge cake, preferably stale
Raspberry/strawberry jam
Strawberries/raspberries tinned or frozen
Sherry (lots of)
Homemade custard using half milk and half cream or whole cream if you're reckless
Whipped cream for topping
Toasted almonds.

Slice the sponge, spread with jam and layer in deep bowl. I like to use a glass one so that you can see all the layers. Pour on sherry. Then pour on some more. Cover with fruit.

Make custard using at least four egg yolks, 500g cream/milk, 40g sugar and vanilla pod.

Heat the cream and vanilla (natural essence will do) then when up to the boil pour it onto the beaten egg yolks and sugar. A teaspoon of flour added to the mixture will prevent it curdling.

Pour back into the pan and slowly reheat until thick. Do not allow to boil.

Pour custard over trifle and allow to cool. Whip up more cream and spread over custard. Toast almonds and sprinkle over shortly before serving.

Vin d'Oranges

4 Seville oranges
5 bottles of rosé wine (12%)
zest of a lemon
2 litres pure fruit alcohol
800g granulated sugar
1 vanilla pod

Cut the oranges into smallish chunks and place in large container which has a tight seal. Add all the remaining ingredients and close firmly. Leave for at least one month, shaking every day. Filter through muslin into clean bottles. Makes approx 6 litres

It improves with age so try not to drink it all at once. Not easy!

Seville Orange Marmalade

Makes about 14 jars

1.5 kilos Seville oranges

3 navel oranges

2 lemons

2.6kg   preserving sugar

3 ¾ litres water

Wash the oranges and lemons and cut them in half, removing all the pips. Cut the halves in two and slice very finely with very sharp knife. (This takes a long time so make yourself comfortable at a large table, pour yourself a drink, or better still get a friend to help). Put in a large pan and pour in the water. Bring to the boil and then reduce heat and simmer for about 1 ½ hours until peel is soft. Add the sugar, stir until dissolved. **Boil rapidly until setting** point is reached (approx 30/40 mins) Pour hot jam into sterilised jars, and put on lids immediately.

Options: Add a little finely chopped crystallised ginger with the sugar.

Bon   Appétit!

Lightning Source UK Ltd.
Milton Keynes UK
12 January 2010

148490UK00001B/3/P